MEET THE AUTHOR

Sally Murphy Morris earned her degree in Home Economics at the University of Wisconsin. In 1972 she began demonstrating the use of microwave ovens. This led to teaching classes, making friends and exchanging ideas with prominent San Francisco Bay Area food authorities and testing literally hundreds of recipes. Her book Microwave Cooking is a collection of the best.

In 1977 Sally's husband was transferred to New Jersey. There, she continued to study a favorite subject of hers, seafood. Soon, she was prompted to write Seafood, which details her considerable knowledge of that subject.

In 1981, yet another transfer brought the Morris family to Honolulu, Hawaii where they currently live.

This transcontinental life nourishes Sally's interest in regional and ethnic foods. Daughters Kathy and Kristy, and husband Dave have also helped to encourage and serve as "taste-testers" over the years. It is hoped that these Morris family favorites will soon become your family's most requested recipes.

AT LAST! A MICROWAVE BOOK THAT MAKES MICROWAVE COOKING EASY

- A wide variety of delicious recipes that can be made easily and quickly in your microwave oven.

- Complete instructions on selecting cooking times, defrosting, reheating and converting recipes for microwave use.

- A chapter especially designed for kids, with quick and easy recipes children can make by themselves.

- Hints on how to melt butter, reheat coffee, warm-up baby's formula, plus other time-savers.

- As with all Nitty Gritty Cookbooks, the recipes are easy to follow and are printed one per page, in large, easy-to-read type.

- For added convenience, this book is uniquely designed to take a minimum of counter space and to keep your place when folded open.

SATISFACTION GUARANTEE — If you are not completely satisfied with any Nitty Gritty book, we will gladly refund your purchase price. Simply return it to us within 30 days along with your receipt.

The author wishes to thank Marion Cunningham, Rhoda Yee, and Ken Wolfe, as well as the many friends who helped contribute recipes and ideas. A special thank you to Jackie Walsh for the opportunity to fulfill a long standing ambition. Finally, thanks to my parents, who cleaned the mess from my first cooking experience at age four, and have encouraged me ever since.

Easy Microwave Cooking

by Sally Murphy Morris

Illustrated by Mike Nelson

© Copyright 1976
Nitty Gritty Productions
P. O. Box 5457
Concord, California 94524-0457

A Nitty Gritty Cookbook
Printed by Mariposa Press
Concord, California

ISBN 0-911954-36-8
Library of Congress Catalog Card Number: 76-3428

Second Edition 1981, completely revised
Twelfth printing 1983

TABLE OF CONTENTS

INTRODUCTION

Many changes have taken place in the kitchen in the past quarter century. Probably none are greater than in the devices used to cook our food. Today's consumer has a choice of conventional, microwave, combination microwave-conventional, convection, and very soon, microwave-convection ovens.

Still the most dramatic and efficient is the microwave oven. Once thought of as a luxury, it is now a necessity in millions of homes. When you thoroughly understand the principles of microwave cooking, you will find the portable microwave oven can do most everything. The exceptions are browning of quickly cooked foods such as cookies, breads and toppings you would normally broil to brown, and reduction of liquids. This is because there is little drying in a microwave environment. The new combination microwave ovens will remedy this, or a conventional broiler can be used briefly on already cooked foods. A word of caution here: if you do pop food under the broiler after microwave cooking, be sure it is on a broiler safe pan.

At the time of the first edition of this book, 1976, there were only two choices of cooking power, high and defrost. Technology has taken us a long way since then. In addition to ten levels of cooking power, new ovens boast such features as pressure sensitive pads in place of dials, digital clocks, built-in temperature probes, permanent recipe programs, revolving turntables, and automatic start times. One manufacturer even provides an optional Braille adaptor kit for the blind.

This edition presents material to reflect the changes in cooking levels. However, if you have an older model oven, you may still use this book. You may have to adjust the times slightly and stir and rotate more frequently, but your results will be comparable.

Before you begin trying recipes, sit down, prop your feet up, and spend an evening reading through the book. A great amount of information, including hints and tips are chocked between the covers. Understand it, put it to good use, and you will be as excited about microwave cooking as I am.

Sally Murphy Morris

MICROWAVE COOKING TIPS

TIMING

Several factors affect cooking time. The first is the watts of cooking power of your oven. Top-of-the-line models generally have 650 to 700 watts output. It is important to know this figure for your oven. If yours does not have at least 650 watts, the recipes in this book will take 1 to 3 minutes longer.

Other factors that affect the timing include the density of the food, the volume to be cooked, the starting temperature of the food, the fat and sugar content, the shape, the moisture content, whether or not it is covered, and the arrangement of the food in the oven. Whenever possible, arrange food in a circle with nothing in the center. If cooking several pieces of something such as chicken, have the thickest parts on the outside. Your oven manual should explain these points in greater detail.

The recipes in this book were kitchen tested in a 650 watt oven.

COOKING POUCHES

Commercially packed or home-filled cooking pouches may be used in a micro-wave oven. Pierce a hole in the bag, before cooking, to allow steam to escape. Place pouch on a small plate. Cook 1/3 of the time recommended for cooking in water. Turn pouch over, half way through the cooking period. Most 10 ounce packages take 6 to 7 minutes.

DO NOT use ordinary plastic bags . . . they will melt! Cooking pouches which can be purchased for home use are made of special nylon or polyester film. Some of the brand names are Glad Oven Bags, Cooking Magic, Reynolds Brown In A Bag and Seal-A-Meal Bags.

DEFROSTING FROZEN VEGETABLES

To defrost frozen vegetables, cut a large X or poke holes in the box or bag. Place in the oven and microwave 4 to 6 minutes. Allow to rest a few minutes. Stir. If necessary, microwave 1 to 2 minutes longer. Drain.

COVERS

New microwave oven owners are often confused as to whether or not a food should be covered. Thinking about what types of coverings are available and what purpose each serves will assist in the decision of which to use.

Self-covers: this is the skin that nature provided on such foods as potatoes, squash, apples and egg yolks. Prick before cooking to allow steam to escape. Caution: never cook eggs in their shells!

Tight-fitting covers: can be a glass lid made to fit a specific dish, an overturned plate, or plastic wrap. Plastic usually needs to be pricked to prevent heated steam from making a balloon. Remove these covers with great care to prevent burns from the hot steam.

Semi-tight covers: are used to hold in heat for more rapid cooking; will allow browning and will help prevent spatters. Waxed paper is the best example.

Loose-fitting covers: can be of paper, such as toweling or napkins, or of cotton or linen fabric, such as a napkin or tea towel. These covers are useful when you want some of the moisture to pass through and some to remain in the food. Bread wrapped in cloth will heat more evenly and stand less chance of drying out and hardening.

REHEATING FOODS

Leftovers are now planned-overs! Since the food doesn't dry out as it would in a conventional oven, you will be delighted to have leftovers for busy day meals. Each plateful of food takes 2 to 3 minutes to return from refrigerated temperature to serving temperature. Remember this handy trick when reheating dinner for latecomers.

Due to the fat content and the thinness of the pieces, meats, poultry,and fish require 1/2 to 1 minute per serving to reheat.

Porous items such as bread, rolls, cakes, pies, etc., need about 10 seconds per serving to heat. Be very careful not to over heat or they will become tough and inedible. They only need to be warm to the touch, not hot.

Dense items such as beverages, soups, casseroles, etc., require about 1-1/2 minutes per serving.

Covering the food you are heating reduces the timing slightly.

Warming baby's formula right in the bottle, either glass or plastic, takes only 30 to 45 seconds for 8 ounces at medium-high (70%) setting. Shake gently to equalize the temperature. Test temperature before feeding.

CONVERTING RECIPES

When you are thoroughly accustomed to the operation of your microwave oven, you will want to try converting your favorite recipes from conventional to shorter microwave cooking times. Not only is this easy to do, but often you will eliminate some of the extra procedures (such as frying before baking), extra dishes and pans, and excessive clean up time.

When a recipe calls for a long baking period, try 1/4 of that time for microwave cooking. If more time is necessary, add the extra time carefully, 30 seconds to 1 minute at a time. Remember that foods continue to cook after being removed from the oven. Roasts, for instance, take 20 minutes to reach their optimum temperatures. Cakes should look fairly dry on top, and also will have pulled away from the sides of the pan.

Keep in mind the importance of stirring, especially for soups, sauces, and vegetables, and of turning, for cakes, meats, and fruits. Even cooking produces a better product.

ABOUT POWER LEVELS

The most frequently asked question from new microwave oven owners is "What temperature do I use?" The answer is: with microwave cooking the temperature setting is eliminated. Instead we speak of volume of food to be cooked and the time to cook that volume. With recent developments, a new dimension is added— level of power. Top of the line models use 650 to 750 watts of power. When the first edition of this book was printed, the choice was for full power or a setting called defrost. Now ovens boast up to ten choices of power levels (although not all manufacturers are using the same terms). Compare the terminology of your oven with the terms used in the following chart:*

TERM	% OF POWER	PROCESS	LEVEL	650 WATT OVEN
HIGH	100%	Full power, Cook	9	650 watts
MEDIUM-HIGH	70%	Roast	7	500 watts
MEDIUM	50%	Simmer or slow	5	325 watts
MEDIUM-LOW	30%	Simmer or defrost	3	200 watts
LOW	10%	Warm	1	65 to 70 watts

*Recommended by the Microwave Power Institute/Cooking Appliance Section

A temperature setting may be used in a microwave oven if the oven is equipped with a built in thermometer probe. This is available in some top-of-the-line models. If your oven has such a probe, check your use and care manual for correct operation. With this option, the probe is placed into the food to be cooked, the degree of doneness is set, and the microwaves cook the food to that setting. When the setting is reached, the oven holds the food at serving temperature.

NOTE: ALL RECIPES IN THIS BOOK USE HIGH OR FULL POWER UNLESS OTHERWISE NOTED. Owners of ovens having only the high setting may use all the recipes given but may find they take a slightly shorter time and may require more stirring at shorter intervals than when a lower setting is used.

KNOW YOUR MICROWAVE OVEN

TESTING YOUR OVEN

If you have a 650 or 700 watt oven, and if you suspect it may not be cooking food as quickly as you feel it should, perform the following tests.

1. Double check your timer with a stopwatch.
2. Measure 1 quart of very warm water from the tap. Record the temperature using a frying, candy or instant reading thermometer. Microwave 2 minutes. The temperature of the water should be 30 to 34 degrees higher than the original temperature.
3. In a darkened room, turn the oven light on. Close the oven. You should see no light around the door.

If you suspect any malfunction of your oven, discontinue use and call your dealer or authorized service organization. They will have special testing equipment to help them locate the problem, if there is one, and make whatever repairs are necessary.

By all means, never let anyone but an authorized serviceman repair your oven. To do so will void the warranty as well as cause more serious problems.

CLEANING YOUR OVEN

It is important to keep a microwave oven clean, particularly around the door seal. Giving the inside of your oven a quick wipe with a soapy cloth or sponge after each use is a good habit. If greasy spatters do build up, it is easy to loosen them by creating steam in the oven. To do this, place an open container with one cup of water in it, in the oven. Microwave 3 to 4 minutes. Wait a few minutes before opening the door. The steam that has been generated will allow you to easily wipe the walls clean. Don't forget the roof of the oven, but be careful if the fan blades are not covered.

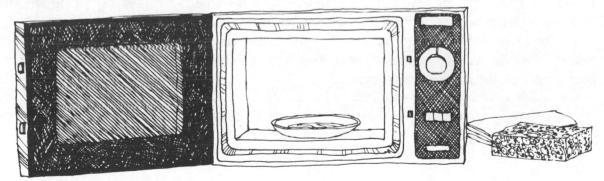

CAUTIONS

Make sure your oven is plugged into an outlet with a ground wire.

If you have small children who might be tempted to play with the oven dials, keep a glass of water in the oven. Then if it is accidentally started, the water will absorb the microwaves. Operating a microwave oven without anything in it can wear out or damage the magnetron tube.

Never attempt to bypass the built-in safety mechanisms.

Popcorn which is popped in a microwave oven is never very satisfactory, but it can even be dangerous if popped in a paper bag. There is always the possibility of the popcorn getting hot enough to set the bag on fire.* Reheating popcorn in a microwave oven, however, gives it a just-popped flavor.

* While several manufacturers have developed corn poppers specifically for the microwave oven, most people believe the best results are obtained when corn is popped by more traditional methods.

> To warm baby food, remove lid from jar of food. Place opened jar in the oven and microwave about 30 seconds. Stir well. Test temperature before serving. If only a small portion is to be used, remove to a microwave-safe dish before serving.

SPECIAL EQUIPMENT

New products are appearing daily to make microwave cooking a breeze. Here are some favorite proven items which no good microwave cook will want to do without.

Four and eight cup measures: Large glass measuring bowls are invaluable for mixing as well as for baking (pudding, soups, Plum Pudding and other cakes).

Scale: Whether countertop or folding wall model, a good scale is an indispensable necessity.

Pans with handles: Handles or wide lips on pans facilitate removal of hot food from the oven.

Instant Reading Thermometer: Remove cooked food from oven, insert this new type of thermometer, and get an instant read out. Watch the temperature rise during the hold-over or resting period.

Clayware: This cookware is useful for fish, poultry, and less tender cuts of meat. Soak lid and bottom with water for 15 minutes before using.

Muffin pans: For muffins, cupcakes and also eggs (if there are no holes in the bottom), these pans may be ceramic or temperature resistant plastic. The circular shape is advantageous for evenly baked muffins.

Bundt pans: Plastic, glass and ceramic are all available for baking cakes and casseroles.

Ring molds: Fine for meat loaves and casseroles. The shape is particularly good for microwave cooking.

Paper containers: Polyester coated heavy paper utensils may be used for freezer to oven cooking. They may also be used in conventional ovens by lowering the temperature 25°. They are non-stick.

Browning skillet or griddle: The tin oxide coating on the bottom absorbs microwaves when the utensil is preheated. When food is added, it browns and sears, just as with a fry pan on a burner.

14

COOKING TIME CHART

You may wish to remove this page and tape it inside a cupboard door over your oven. ALL TIMES LISTED ARE FOR HIGH POWER WITH 650 WATT OVEN. If your oven is 700 to 750 watts, you will need slightly less time. Ovens with less than 600 watts will need slightly more. Compare these times with the times given in your manual.

Bacon	1/2 to 1 min. per slice
Beef, ground	5 to 6 min. per lb.
meatloaf	6 to 7 min. per lb.
patties	5 min. per lb.
roast	7 to 9 min. per lb. (rare) 10 to 11 min. per lb. (medium)
	12 to 13 min. per lb. (well)
Beverages	1 to 2 min. per cup
Cakes, bundt	9 to 13 min.
cupcakes	1–1/2 to 2 min. per 6 cakes
layer	5 to 6 min. per layer
upside-down	6 to 7 min. per cake

Casseroles	5 to 7 min. per quart
Crust crumb	1–1/2 to 2–1/2 min. per 9" crust
pastry	4 to 5 min. per 9" crust
Eggs	1/2 to 3/4 min. per egg
Fish	4 min. per lb.
Lamb, chops	5 to 6 min. per lb.
leg	7 to 9 min. per lb. (medium) 10 to 12 min. per lb. (well done)
roast	9 to 10 min. per lb.
Meatloaf	10 min. per lb.
Muffins	2 to 3 min. per 6 muffins
Pork, chops	8 to 10 min. per 4 medium chops
roast	9 to 10 min. per lb.
sausage	8 to 9 min. per lb.
Ham, boneless	10 to 12 min. per lb. (over 5 lb., 7 to 8 min. per lb.)
slice	7 min. per lb.
whole	6 min. per lb.
Poultry, chicken	7 to 8 min. per lb.

turkey	6 min. per lb.
Sandwiches	1/2 min. per sandwich
Sauces	2 to 3 min. per cup
Veal (all)	7 to 8 min. per lb.
Vegetables, canned	1 to 2 min. per cup
frozen	6 to 9 min. per 10 oz. pkg.
fresh	6 to 9 min. per lb., see below

4 min. per lb. (slightly less per pound if cooking large quantity). Artichokes, beets, two carrots, three celery sticks, two ears of corn, small eggplant, mushrooms, peas, potatoes,

7 to 9 min. per lb.

asparagus, beets, bell pepper, broccoli, brussel sprouts, cabbage, cauliflower, celery (4 cups), onions, parsnips, peas, rutabagas, spinach, summer squash (2 medium),

12 to 14 min. per lb.

beans (green, wax, French cut), squash (acorn, butternut)

APPETIZERS

Appetizers are fun and super-quick in a microwave oven. All of the recipes in this chapter are equally suitable for family snacks or for entertaining.

For easy parties, plan ahead. Most of the recipes can be assembled early in the day, wrapped in plastic wrap or waxed paper and refrigerated. To serve, pop them into the oven and in seconds they are ready.

To introduce your microwave oven to guests, mark the cooking time on each recipe and they will enjoy being guest chefs. Children and husbands can be helpful in this way, too.

Melba rounds and Triscuits are recommended as foundations for individual appetizers. To heat the appetizers, arrange in a circle, six or eight to a plate. Microwave 20 to 25 seconds (45 seconds if frozen) per plateful.

Cheese melts perfectly and is easily reheated so it is an excellent choice for appetizers of all descriptions. If you have variable power settings, it is best to use a medium (50%) or medium-low (30%) setting for cheese. The timing will be about the same.

PECAN SPREAD

Men really go for this unbelievably easy dip.

1 pkg. (8 ozs.) cream cheese
2 tbs. milk
1/4 cup finely chopped green pepper
1/2 tsp. garlic salt
1/4 tsp. pepper

2 tbs. dry onion flakes
1/2 cup sour cream
1 tbs. butter, melted
1/2 cup coarsely chopped pecans
1/2 tsp. salt

Put cream cheese in a large soup bowl or small casserole suitable for serving. Microwave 45 seconds on low (10%) power or just until softened. Add milk, green pepper, garlic salt, pepper, onion flakes and sour cream. Mix well. Place butter in a cup. Microwave 30 seconds on medium (50%) power to melt. Add nuts and salt. Stir well. Spoon over cheese mixture. Serve at room temperature or microwave about 1 minute on high (100%) power to serve warm. Serve with a variety of crackers or firm chips. Makes 2 cups.

QUICK FONDUE

This is perfect with a large plate of fresh vegetables, cubes of French bread or English muffins.

2 cans (10-3/4 ozs. ea.) cheddar cheese soup
1/2 cup dry white wine
1 tsp. Worcestershire sauce
1/4 cup catsup

Put all ingredients into a small casserole. Microwave 3 minutes, on medium (50%) power, stirring often. Whip with a wire whisk if necessary to make very smooth. Transfer to fondue pot to keep hot, or microwave 30 seconds to reheat. Makes about 3 cups.

> To melt butter, place desired amount in a cup or bowl and microwave on medium (50%) power.
> 1 to 4 tablespoons — 15 seconds
> 1/4 to 1/2 cup — 30 to 45 seconds
> 1/2 to 1 cup — 45 to 60 seconds

HOT SHRIMP DIP

Shrimply delicious!

1 clove garlic
1 can (10-3/4 ozs.) shrimp soup, undiluted
1/2 lb. Swiss cheese, grated
2 tbs. sherry

Rub a bowl with garlic. Put soup, cheese and sherry into bowl without mixing. Microwave on medium (50%) power 1 minute. Stir. Microwave 1 to 2 minutes longer, on medium (50%) power until very hot. Serve immediately. If necessary to reheat after being served, cover with a paper towel or waxed paper. Microwave 1 to 2 minutes on low (10%) power depending on the quantity remaining in the bowl. Makes about 1-1/2 cups.

CHEESY CLAM DIP

Even clam-haters will love this.

1 can (7 ozs.) minced clams
2 jars (5 ozs ea.) cheese spread <u>or</u> 1 cup sharp cheddar, grated
1/4 cup green onion, chopped fine
dash garlic powder
1 tsp. Worcestershire sauce
1 tsp. dried parsley flakes
1 tbs. chopped ripe olives
crisp corn chips

Drain off about half of the clam juice. Combine all ingredients except chips in a small casserole or large soup bowl. Stir well. Microwave 2-1/2 minutes on medium (50%) power, stirring often. Serve with chips. To reheat as needed, cover with a paper towel to prevent spattering, and microwave 1 minute or less. Makes about 1-1/2 cups.

EGGPLANT DIP

This unusual flavor is pleasing when combined with raw vegetables. Vary it by adding a cup of ground walnuts.

1 medium eggplant	1 tomato, minced
1/2 tsp. allspice	2 tsp. instant onion
1/2 tsp. garlic salt	2 tbs. salad oil
1/2 tsp. salt	juice of 1/2 lemon

Wash eggplant and cut off the green cap. Poke the skin in several places with a fork. Place on a paper plate and microwave 7 to 8 minutes, on high (100%) power, turning plate 180º half way through cooking time. Most of the skin will turn from purple to brown and will feel soft. Allow to cool. Cut in half. Scoop insides into a blender container. Add remaining ingredients. Cover and blend 3 to 4 minutes. Serve chilled with raw vegetables for dipping. Makes 1–1/2 cups.

To recrisp chips and crackers, microwave on high (100%) power, 45 seconds to 1 minute per plateful.

CHILI DIP

Keep the ingredients handy on your pantry shelf and treat unexpected guests to something special.

1 can (15 ozs.) chili con carne without beans
1 jar (8 ozs.) Cheez Whiz
1 tbs. taco seasoning (optional)

Place chili and cheese in a glass serving dish. Microwave 2 minutes on medium (50%) power until cheese is melted. Stir. Serve with tortilla chips. Reheats easily, but cover with plastic wrap or paper towels to prevent spatters. Makes about 3 cups.

ARTICHOKE SQUARES

Make early in the day and reheat when needed.

2 jars (6 ozs. ea.) marinated artichoke hearts
1/2 cup green onion, finely chopped
1 clove garlic, minced
4 eggs, slightly beaten
1/2 cup dried bread crumbs
1/2 tsp. salt

1/4 tsp. each, pepper and basil
1/2 tsp. oregano
1/2 lb. sharp cheddar or Monterey
    Jack cheese, grated
1/2 cup Parmesan cheese, grated

Drain marinade from 1 jar of artichokes into an 8 x 8-inch glass pan or 9-inch Corning skillet. Discard marinade from second jar. Add onion and garlic to skillet. Cover. Microwave 1–1/2 minutes on high (100%) power. Spoon off excess oil and moisture. Chop artichoke hearts. In a small bowl, beat eggs. Add chopped artichokes, crumbs, seasonings, and cheeses. Add to onion. Microwave 4 to 5 minutes on high (100%) power, until just set. Stir occasionally during the first 3 minutes. Cool. Cut into 1-inch squares. Serve cold, or reheat one minute. Makes about 60 servings.

COTTAGE MUSHROOMS

Low in calories but high in taste pleasure, you'll see mushroom skeptics return for seconds.

16 large mushrooms
1 tsp. water
1-1/2 tbs. green onion, finely sliced
2 tsp. butter

1/2 tsp. Worcestershire sauce
1/2 cup small curd cottage cheese
salt and pepper to taste
1/2 cup grated Parmesan cheese

Wash mushrooms. Pull out stems and chop them. Put mushroom caps on a glass plate. Sprinkle with water. Cover with plastic wrap. Microwave 1-1/2 minutes. Drain and pat backs with paper towel. Combine chopped stems, onion and butter in a small bowl. Cover with plastic wrap. Microwave 1 minute. Add remaining ingredients. Stuff caps. Place on an ovenproof platter. Broil in conventional oven until light brown. Makes 16.

CHEESE DIPPED PRETZELS

A great hit with all ages. Let the children help make them.

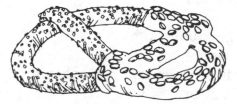

1 pkg. (8 ozs.) process American cheese
1/2 cup light cream
1/2 tsp. Tabasco sauce
1 pkg. pretzels
1 tbs. poppy seeds <u>or</u> toasted sesame seeds

Cut cheese into cubes. Put cubes, cream and Tabasco into a casserole. Microwave 2 to 3 minutes on medium (50%) power, stirring often, until cheese is melted. Dip half of each pretzel into cheese and then sprinkle with seeds. Place on waxed paper until firm. Quantity depends on pretzel size.

SPINACH TART

A delightful appetizer that also makes a delicious side dish.

2 tbs. butter
1/4 ts. basil
1/4 tsp. oregano
1 small onion, finely chopped
2 cups shredded fresh spinach
1 tbs. all-purpose flour

1 cup shredded cheese, Monterey Jack,
    Muenster, or Cheddar
1 can (5 ozs.) evaporated milk
4 eggs, beaten
pinch nutmeg
pinch cayenne pepper
1 tsp. salt

Place butter in a glass cake or pie pan. Cook on medium-high (70%) power until melted, about 30 seconds. Add basil, oregano and onion. Cook 1 minute on high (100%) power. Add spinach. Cook 1 minute on high power. Mix together flour and cheese. Add remaining ingredients. Stir into onion mixture. Cook on medium power (50%) for 12 minutes, stirring after six minutes. Remove from oven. Allow to stand 10 minutes before serving. Makes 10 to 12 servings.

SOUPS AND SAUCES

Soups and sauces are extremely quick and easy to make in a microwave oven, and scorching is never a problem because liquids cook from all sides.

Prepare, cook and serve family-sized quantities of soup in a tureen or casserole. Reheat as needed by microwaving a minute or two.

Individual servings are easily made right in soup bowls or mugs. Spoon the contents of a ten ounce can of condensed soup into two or three mugs or bowls. Add milk or water and stir. Microwave 2 minutes per serving. Stir again and serve.

When making sauces be sure to stir frequently. If they contain egg yolks, do not boil.

Sauces thickened with cornstarch, arrowroot or flour should be allowed to boil for one minute to eliminate the uncooked flavor of starch.

A 1-quart glass measure is excellent for sauce making. It is large enough to prevent most boil-overs and is handy for pouring.

Many sauces will continue to cook and often will thicken more, after being removed from the oven.

CHEDDAR CREAM SOUP

Nutritious and satisfying for a bleak day. Serve icy cold on a warm day.

1/4 cup butter
1/2 onion, finely minced
1/4 cup all-purpose flour
1 tsp. salt
1/4 tsp. pepper
4 cups milk
3 cups grated extra sharp cheddar cheese

Put butter and onion in a large casserole and microwave 5 minutes. Add the flour, salt, pepper and milk. Stir well. Microwave 8 minutes, stirring a few times, until mixture just begins to boil. Add cheese. Microwave 2 to 3 minutes until cheese is melted. Blend thoroughly. Garnish with parsley or chives, if desired. Makes 6 servings.

VICHYSOISSE

Delightful served well chilled on a warm day, but pleasing served hot as well.

2 tbs. butter
2 bunches leeks (6 to 8), chopped
1 onion, chopped
4 potatoes, peeled and cubed
2 cups chicken stock

2 chicken bouillon cubes
1 tsp. Spice Islands Beau Monde Seasoning
salt and cayenne pepper to taste
2 cups (1 pt.) light cream
chopped chives

Melt butter in a large casserole with a cover. Add leeks and onions. Cover. Microwave 5 minutes. Add potatoes, stock and seasonings. Microwave 6 to 8 minutes until the potatoes are cooked. Cool slightly. Puree in blender. Pour into large bowl or pitcher. Stir in cream. Correct seasonings. Chill. To serve, garnish with chives. Makes 8 servings.

TOMATO BISQUE

A perfect warmer-upper for chilly evenings.

2 cups tomato juice
2 cups beef consomme
1 tbs. sherry for each serving (optional)
sour cream
chives

Combine juice and consomme. Add sherry, if desired. Pour into four mugs. Microwave 1–1/2 minutes for each serving. Garnish with sour cream and chives. Makes 4 servings.
Note: Tomato Bisque can be made in any amount desired. Just mix the juice and consomme in equal amounts. Save dishes by mixing right in the mugs.

> Stir a package of Lipton's Cup-A-Soup into a cup or mug of water. Microwave 1–1/2 to 2 minutes. Stir again before serving.

EASY BARBEQUE SAUCE

Make this ahead and store up to a week, lightly covered, in the refrigerator.

1 cup catsup
2 cups water
1 tsp. salt
1 tsp chili powder
1/4 tsp. Worcestershire sauce
1/2 cup minced onion

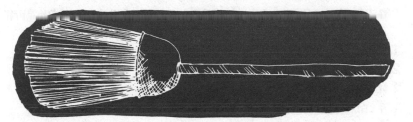

Blend all ingredients in a 4-cup glass measure. Microwave 5 minutes. It thickens slightly as it cooks more as it cools. To use, pour over browned meat—beef patties, beef roast, short ribs, pork shops, lamb chops—or brush liberally over browned chicken pieces. Cook until tender. Baste occasionally during remaining cooking time. Makes 3 cups.

HOLLANDAISE SAUCE

At last! An easy way to make this classic sauce. Hollandaise, the most necessary ingredient for Eggs Benedict, is also delicious with asparagus, broccoli, cauliflower and fish. Stir often so the eggs cook evenly.

1/4 cup butter
2 egg yolks
1 tbs. lemon juice
1/4 tsp. salt
1/4 tsp. dry mustard

Put butter into a 2-cup glass measure. Microwave 30 seconds to melt. Add egg yolks and whip well with a wire whisk. Add the remaining ingredients and whip until well mixed. Microwave 1 minute, stirring often. Overcooking will curdle the eggs. If this occurs, beat in 1 tablespoon of cold milk or light cream. Serve warm. To reheat, microwave 30 to 35 seconds, stirring often. Makes 2/3 cup sauce.

MORNAY SAUCE

Marvelous with fish, eggs, vegetables, chicken and meats. Serve it often, it's so easy with a microwave oven.

2 tbs. butter
2 tbs. all-purpose flour
1/3 cup milk
1 cup water
1 cube or 1 tsp. chicken bouillon
1/4 cup grated Parmesan cheese
1/4 cup shredded Swiss cheese

Put butter into a 2-cup glass measure. Microwave 15 seconds to melt. Stir in flour, then milk, water and bouillon. Microwave 2 to 3 minutes until mixture bolls, stirring often after the first minute. Stir in cheeses. Cover until the cheeses melt. Serve warm. Makes 1–2/3 cups.

MEDIUM WHITE SAUCE

Many recipes begin with a medium white sauce. Now making it in a microwave oven is foolproof and quick.

2 tbs. butter or margarine   1/2 tsp. salt   1 cup milk
2 tbs. all-purpose flour   dash pepper

Place butter in a 2-cup glass measure. Microwave 45 seconds until melted. Stir in flour, salt and pepper. Add milk. Microwave 2-1/2 to 3-1/2 minutes until boiling, stirring a few times after the first minute. Makes 1 cup.

For 2 cups of white sauce, use a glass, 4-cup measure and double the ingredients. Microwave 5 to 6 minutes.

CHEESE SAUCE

Add 1/4 teaspoon dry mustard with the flour. After sauce has cooked and thickened, stir in 1/2 to 1 cup shredded cheese until melted.

MUSTARD SAUCE

This piquant sauce gives ham or vegetables a touch of class. It reheats nicely.

2 eggs, slightly beaten
1/4 cup sugar
2 to 3 tsp. dry mustard
1/4 cup milk
1/4 cup white vinegar
2 tbs. butter

Put all ingredients into a 2-cup glass measure or pretty pitcher. Stir with a whisk. Microwave 2–3/4 minutes on medium (50%) power, stirring several times after the first minute, until mixture just comes to a boil and is thick. Be sure to stir often to prevent the egg white from being cooked too quickly. Makes 1 cup.

Always cook fresh vegetables with a cover, except those cooked with their skins on. A fitted glass lid or plastic wrap stretched tightly over the dish hastens cooking.

SWEET AND SOUR SAUCE

Serve with won ton, meat balls, small ribs or pork.

1 can (15–1/2 ozs.) crushed pineapple
2 tbs. cornstarch
1/2 cup brown sugar
2 tsp. salt
1/3 cup vinegar
2 tbs. catsup
1 tsp. Worcestershire sauce

Drain pineapple into a 4-cup glass measure or glass bowl. Stir corn starch into juice. Add all ingredients except the pineapple. Microwave 3-1/2 minutes, stirring every 30 seconds until thickened and clear. Add crushed pineapple. Microwave 1/2 minute longer. If too thick, thin with any fruit juice or water. Serve warm. Makes 2 cups.

CREAMY SAUCE FOR FRUIT

Good for a fresh or canned fruit salad. Also, try it on slices of cake or layered with fruit gelatin in parfait glasses.

1 pkg. (3 ozs.) French vanilla pudding mix
1 cup fruit juice (orange, pineapple, cranberry)

Mix in a pitcher or measuring cup. Microwave 3-1/2 to 4 minutes until thickened. Cool. Makes 1 cup.

SOUR CREAM SAUCE

1 cup (1/2 pt.) sour cream   1/2 tsp. garlic salt
1/4 cup tomato sauce

Combine in a 2-cup glass measure or pretty pitcher. Microwave 2 minutes on medium (50%) power, until heated through. Do not boil. Makes 1-1/4 cups.

LEMON SAUCE

Serve over gingerbread, sponge cake or fruit.

1/2 cup sugar
1 tbs. cornstarch
1 cup warm water
2 tbs. butter or margarine
zest of 1 lemon
juice of 1 lemon

In a 2-cup glass measure, combine sugar and cornstarch. Stir until well mixed. Add water. Microwave 2 to 3 minutes. Stir every 30 seconds, until mixture has thickened and boiled for 30 seconds. Watch carefully so that it does not boil over. Add butter, zest (very outer rind without the pith), and juice. Serve warm or cold. Makes 1–1/2 cups.

Soften unflavored gelatine in cold water in a glass measure, then microwave until bubbly, to dissolve.

GOLDEN SAUCE

Little people may not like plum pudding, but you can be sure they will ask for seconds when this delicious sauce tops it.

1/2 cup butter
1-1/4 cups sugar
5 tbs. cream
1 egg, beaten
1 tsp. vanilla

Place butter in a glass bowl and microwave 10 seconds. Wait 10 seconds, then microwave 5 seconds more. The butter should just be soft, not melted. Using an electric mixer, gradually beat in the sugar, then add cream and egg. Microwave 3-1/2 to 4 minutes, on medium (50%) power, stirring every 30 seconds. Stir in vanilla. Serve over English Plum Pudding, page 138. Pass extra sauce for those with a sweet tooth. Makes about 2 cups.

CARAMEL SAUCE

Great over ice cream and for Pappy's Special Angel Torte on page 156!

5 tbs. butter
1 cup brown sugar
1/4 cup milk, evaporated milk, or cream*
1/2 tsp. vanilla
2 tbs. white corn syrup

Combine ingredients in a 2 or 4-cup glass measure. Microwave 2 minutes on medium (50%) power. Stir hard to blend. This sauce thickens as it cools. Reheat 30 to 45 seconds. Avoid overheating as it will cause the sauce to sugar. Makes 1 cup.
*When making this sauce for Pappy's Dessert, page 156, you can "borrow" 1/4 cup whipping cream from the dessert ingredients, decreasing the amount of cream used in Pappy's Dessert to 3/4 cup.

> To help make timing less critical and prevent sugar crystals from forming in sweet sauces, add 2 tablespoons white corn syrup for each cup of sugar used.

CRIMSON RASPBERRY SAUCE

A most delightful way to top cheesecake, poached fruit or ice cream.

1 pkg. (10 ozs.) frozen red raspberries
2 tsp. cornstarch
1/2 cup currant jelly

To thaw berries, remove metal ends from the carton and push the berries out into a glass bowl. Microwave 1 to 2 minutes until just barely thawed. Crush by hand or in blender. Put back into small glass bowl. Add cornstarch and jelly. Microwave 3 minutes, stirring every half minute until clear and slightly thick. Strain to remove seeds. Cool. Makes 1–1/4 cups.

HOT FUDGE SAUCE

This is a lovely dark, rich sauce that does not become hard and brittle when served over ice cream. It keeps for weeks in the refrigerator and can be reheated by microwaving 30 to 60 seconds.

2 tbs. butter or margarine
1 cup whipping cream
1 cup sugar
pinch of salt
4 squares (4 ozs.) unsweetened chocolate

Combine everything except the chocolate in a 4-cup glass measuring cup. Microwave 2 minutes. Stir. Microwave 2 minutes more until sugar is completely dissolved. Add chocolate. Microwave 2 minutes or until chocolate is melted. Stir until smooth. Serve hot, warm or at room temperature.

MEAT ENTREES

While the recipes in this section take an hour or more to cook conventionally, you can usually prepare them in your microwave oven in fifteen minutes or less. They have been family tested and are popular with guests as well. Should there be leftovers, you may reheat them, assured that they will lose none of their original flavor or texture.

Whenever possible, stir the ingredients as they cook, to assist in more even cooking. After being removed from the oven, cover cooked food with plastic wrap, a lid, or upturned plate. This will contain the heat until you are ready to serve.

If a casserole has been assembled early in the day and refrigerated, remember to add about two minutes to the cooking time.

Because large quantities of water usually require a long cooking time, it is usually easiest to cook rice and pasta by conventional methods.

FRENCH DIP SANDWICHES

Perfect for after a football game or tennis match. While the *au jus* heats, toss a big green salad.

1 sirloin tip roast (2 to 4 lbs.)
1 pkg. (1 oz.) Shilling Au Jus Mix
water
small crusty dinner rolls
butter
mustard, mayonnaise, horseradish

Early in the day, or the day before, place roast in a glass pan. Microwave 6 minutes per pound for medium rare. Rest. The cooking will continue and the temperature will rise about 20 degrees during this time. Cool completely, reserving the drippings. Slice roast very thinly when cold. Pour au jus mix and drippings into a 4-cup glass measure. Fill to the 3-cup mark with water. When ready to serve, butter rolls and fill with meat. Microwave au jus mixture 4 minutes. Place filled rolls in a clean kitchen towel and microwave, allowing 10 to 15 seconds for each roll. Pour au

jus into small, individual serving bowls, giving one to each person. Pass mustard, mayonnaise and horseradish with sandwiches, allowing each person to embellish his own before dipping it into the au jus. Makes 8 to 12 servings.

For tasty croutons cut leftover French bread into small cubes. Place on a paper plate and cover with a paper towel. Microwave 1 to 2 minutes, depending on quantity. Drying will continue after they are removed from the oven.

MEAT LOAF

This hearty favorite will be equally good the second time around, reheated in your microwave oven.

1-1/2 lbs. ground beef	salt, pepper
3/4 lb. ground pork	1/4 tsp. garlic powder
1/2 pkg. onion soup mix	1/2 tsp. Spice Islands Spaghetti Sauce Seasoning
1/2 cup V-8 or tomato juice	6 soda crackers, crushed

Combine all ingredients. Press mixture into a 9 x 5-inch glass loaf pan. If desired, equal parts of water and Kitchen Bouquet may be brushed on the top of loaf for more browning. Cover with waxed paper. Microwave 18 minutes, turning 1/4 turn every five minutes. After ten minutes drain excess juices. If desired, spread catsup over top the last five minutes. Let rest five minutes before serving. Makes 6 to 8 servings.

FAVORITE STUFFED PEPPERS

Delicious, and you'll love the sauce. For variety, fill large tomatoes instead of green peppers.

3 large green peppers	1/2 cup tomato sauce
1 lb. ground beef	1 tsp. salt
1/3 cup rolled oats	1/4 tsp. pepper
1 egg	1/4 tsp. oregano
2 tbs. minced onion	Sour Cream Sauce, page 41

Wash peppers. Cut in half lengthwise. Remove core and seeds. Arrange in a 8 x 12-inch glass baking dish. Add 1/4 cup water. Cover tightly with plastic wrap. Microwave 4 minutes, turning dish after 2 minutes. Combine remaining ingredients in a 1-quart casserole. Microwave 7 to 8 minutes until meat is cooked. Lightly fill the peppers. Arrange in a 8 x 12-inch baking dish. Add 1/4 cup water. Cover with plastic wrap. Microwave 10 minutes. Serve with Sour Cream Sauce. Makes 4 to 6 servings.

POOR MAN'S STROGANOFF

Faster and less expensive than the standard version, this one lacks nothing in flavor. Cook noodles or rice conventionally.

1 lb. ground beef
1 small onion, chopped
1 can (10-3/4 ozs.) cream of mushroom soup, undiluted
1 can (4 ozs.) mushrooms with juice
1/2 tsp. instant beef bouillon
1 cup (1/2 pt.) sour cream or sour half and half

Crumble beef into a 1-1/2quart casserole. Add onion. Microwave, uncovered, 6 minutes. Drain off as much fat as possible. Add remaining ingredients, stirring well. Cover. Microwave 7 to 8 minutes until heated through. Serve over noodles or rice. Makes 4 to 5 servings.

ZUCCHINIBURGER CASSEROLE

This mildly flavored casserole satisfies hearty appetites.

1 lb. ground beef
1/2 tsp. garlic powder
1 medium onion, chopped
1 lb. zucchini, sliced thin
2 cups cooked rice
2 cups (1 pt.) cottage cheese

1 can (10-3/4 ozs.) cream of
    mushroom soup, undiluted
1 tsp. salt
1 cup (4 ozs.) grated sharp cheddar cheese
1/2 cup grated Parmesan cheese

Place beef, garlic powder and onion in a 2-quart casserole. Microwave 5 minutes, stirring after 3 minutes. Drain fat. Add zucchini, rice, cottage cheese, soup and salt. Mix well. Sprinkle cheddar and Parmesan cheeses over the top. Cover. Microwave 8 minutes until bubbly. This also reheats nicely. Makes 5 to 6 servings.

> When removing plastic wrap used to cover a dish during cooking be sure to pierce a hole in it first with a knife to prevent being burned by the steam.

HAMBURGER CASSEROLE LINDGREN

A meat loaf-like family favorite that is prepared in a jiffy.

2 eggs
2 slices white bread, cut in 1/2-inch cubes
1 lb. ground beef
1/4 cup milk
1/4 tsp. pepper
1 tsp. salt
1 can (17 ozs.) cream-style corn
1 tbs. prepared mustard
1 medium onion, chopped

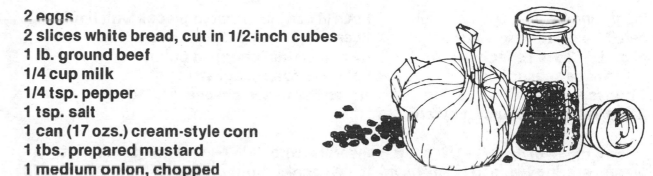

Break eggs into a 1-1/2 quart casserole. Beat slightly with a fork. Add remaining ingredients. Mix to blend. Microwave about 14 minutes, or until firm. During the 14 minute cooking time, stir and turn after 4 minutes, 6 minutes and 8 minutes of cooking. Let rest five minutes before serving. Makes 6 servings.

EASY SPAGHETTI

The tangy sauce belies its ease of preparation.

1 lb. ground beef
1 can (15 ozs.) tomato sauce
1 pkg. (1–1/2 ozs.) spaghetti
    sauce seasoning
1/2 cup red wine
1/2 cup V-8, tomato juice, or water

1 can (4 ozs.) mushroom pieces with liquid
1 can (4-1/2 ozs.) chopped ripe olives
1/2 cup instant chopped onions
1 pkg. (16 ozs.) spaghetti
grated Parmesan cheese

Put meat in to a 2-1/2 quart casserole with lid. Microwave 5 minutes, uncovered, stirring twice to break up meat as it cooks. Pour off accumulated fat. Stir in seasoning, wine, juice, mushrooms, onions and olives. Cover. Microwave 5 minutes, stirring once or twice. To reheat if not used immediately, microwave for 2 minutes. Cook spaghetti conventionally. Serve sauce over spaghetti. Sprinkle with Parmesan cheese. Makes 6 servings.

PIZZA FONDUE

A favorite with children, and big people too. Serve with a molded or tos[ ]
green salad. Quick, easy and very filling.

1/2 lb. ground beef
1/2 cup chopped onion
2 cans (10–1/2 ozs. ea.) pizza
    sauce with cheese
1 tbs. cornstarch
1/2 tsp. basil

2 tsp. oregano
1/4 tsp. garlic powder
2 cups (8 ozs.) grated cheddar cheese
1 cup (4 ozs.) grated Mozzarella cheese
1 loaf French bread, cubed

Crumble beef into a 2-quart casserole. Add onion. Microwave 5 minute[s]
ring after 3 minutes. Drain off fat. Add cornstarch and seasonings to pizza s[ ]
Stir well. Add to meat. Microwave 4 minutes. Mix cheeses. Add to sauce mixt[ ]
at a time. Microwave 1 minute after each addition. Stir well. Serve with bread [ ]
This may be reheated as necessary or transferred to a fondue pot or chafi[ ]
and served immediately. Makes 4 to 6 servings.

CLAY COOKER STEW

If you have a clay cooking pot, you'll find it useful in your microwave oven. Fill the lid and bowl with water and soak for 15 minutes before cooking.

2 tbs. all-purpose flour
1 tsp. dried thyme, crushed
1/2 tsp. salt
1/8 tsp. pepper
1 pkg. (3/4 oz.) instant
   mushroom gravy mix
1 lb. stewing beef, cut into 1-inch cubes

1 cup beef broth or water
1/2 cup dry red wine
1 tsp. Worcestershire sauce
3 medium potatoes, cut into 1-inch cubes
3 carrots, scraped and cut
   into 1-inch pieces
2 stalks celery, cut into 1-inch pieces

Place flour, thyme, salt, pepper and gravy mix in a brown bag or bowl with a cover. Shake to mix. Add beef cubes and shake. Place all in a soaked and drained clay cooking pot. Combine broth, wine and Worcestershire sauce. Pour over meat. Cover and microwave on medium (50%) power for 20 minutes. Add vegetables, tucking under meat. Cover and microwave on medium (50%) power for 45 to 50 minutes more, stirring after 20 minutes. Makes 4 servings.

TACO CASSEROLE

For variety, add a few sliced mushrooms or use Monterey Jack cheese instead of cheddar, or add a small can of corn niblets.

1 lb. ground beef
1/2 cup chopped onion
1 can (8 ozs.) tomato sauce
1 tbs. chili powder
1/2 tsp. salt

1/4 tsp. pepper
1 cup (4 ozs.) grated cheddar cheese
6 corn tortillas, torn into pieces
1 can (2-1/4 ozs.) chopped ripe olives

Place beef in a 2-quart casserole. Microwave 5 minutes, stirring after 3 minutes. Drain. In a large measuring cup or small bowl, mix together onion, tomato sauce, chili powder, salt and pepper. Cover tightly with plastic wrap. Microwave 5 minutes. Stir in meat. Layer tortillas, sauce, cheese and olives in a 2-quart casserole. Microwave 5 to 8 minutes, until cheese is melted and the mixture is very hot. Let rest 5 minutes before serving. (This dish is even better if assembled early in the day and microwaved just before serving.) Makes 4 to 6 servings.

QUICK TAMALE PIE

Chopped fresh tomatoes add a nice tangy flavor, if desired, and a prepared corn bread mix can be used when time is short. Ground chuck has the best fat content for this recipe.

1-1/2 lbs. ground chuck
1 can chopped onion
1 can (10-3/4 ozs.) tomato soup, undiluted
1 tsp. salt
1/2 to 1 tbs. chili powder
1 can (2-1/4 ozs.) sliced ripe olives, drained
1 can (8-3/4 ozs.) whole-kernel corn, well drained
Corn Bread Topping, page 63

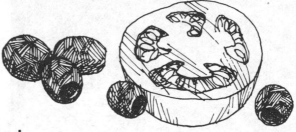

Crumble meat into a large casserole with a lid. Add onions. Microwave 5 to 7 minutes, until meat loses its red color. Stir after 4 minutes. Drain off as much fat as possible. Mix in soup, salt, pepper, chili powder, olives and corn. Cover. Microwave 5 minutes. Meanwhile, prepare Corn Bread Topping. Drop by spoonfuls over hot meat mixture. Cover. Microwave 5 minutes, until bread is baked. Let rest a few minutes before serving. Makes 6 to 8 servings.

CORN BREAD TOPPING

1/2 cup yellow corn meal
1/2 cup all-purpose flour
1 egg
1 tsp. baking powder
1/4 tsp. salt
1 tbs. sugar
1/2 cup milk
2 tbs. salad oil

Mix ingredients together. Use as directed in Quick Tamale Pie recipe.

VEAL PARMIGIANA

Assemble early, cover with waxed paper and refrigerate. At dinnertime, microwave the stated time plus two minutes. For variety try with beef round steak.

1 lb. veal round
1 tbs. butter or margarine
1 tbs. salad oil
1/2 cup crushed cornflakes or crackers
1/4 cup grated Parmesan cheese
1/2 tsp. salt
1 egg, slightly beaten
4 large or 8 small slices cheese, Monterey Jack or mozzarella
1 can (8 ozs.) tomato sauce
1/2 tsp. oregano
1/2 tsp. thyme
1/2 tsp. onion salt

Cut veal into 4 or 5 pieces. Pound with a meat hammer or the edge of a saucer until 1/4-inch thick. Heat butter and oil in a large skillet on top of the range. While this is heating, mix together cracker crumbs, Parmesan cheese and salt. Dip meat into egg, then crumb mixture. Fry in hot butter-oil until golden on both sides. Remove pieces to an 8 x 12-inch glass pan. Scrape drippings from skillet onto chops. Arrange cheese slices over meat. Stir remaining ingredients together. Spoon over cheese. Cover with waxed paper. Microwave 6 minutes. Uncover. Sprinkle with more Parmesan cheese. Microwave 1 minute longer. Makes 4 to 5 servings.

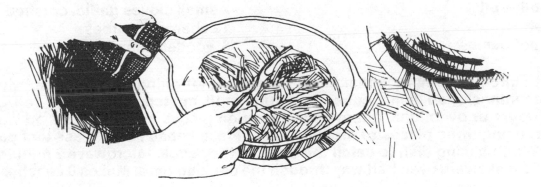

SHISH KEBABS

Cumin adds a very special, earthy flavor.

2 lbs. boneless lamb (leg or shoulder)
1 medium onion, quartered
1 tbs. lemon juice
1/4 cup dry white wine
1/4 cup olive oil
1 tsp. salt
1/8 tsp. pepper

1/2 tsp. oregano
1/2 tsp. cumin seed
1/2 tsp. ground allspice
1 bay leaf, crumbled
2 small cloves garlic, crushed
12 cherry tomatoes
8 wooden skewers

Cut lamb into 2-inch cubes. Make a marinade of onion, lemon juice, wine, oil and seasonings. Add lamb cubes and turn until coated. Cover and refrigerate several hours or overnight. Alternate lamb, onion pieces and tomatoes on wooden skewers, using three pieces of meat for each. Place kebabs over glass loaf pans or an 8 x 12-inch baking dish to catch the drips as they cook. Microwave 2 minutes per kebab. Turn skewers over, half way through the cooking time. Makes 8 kebabs.

LAMB STEW

Lamb and pork are tender meats, and either one may be used for this recipe. If you use pork, then use a dry white wine in place of the red.

1 lb. cubed boneless lamb	2 tsp. Worcestershire sauce
1 pkg. (3/4 oz.) brown gravy mix	1 tbs. lemon juice
2 tbs. all-purpose flour	1 cup chicken broth
1 tsp. garlic salt	1/2 cup dry red wine
1/2 tsp. thyme	3 medium carrots, cut in 1/2-inch pieces
1/2 tsp. celery salt	2 stalks celery, cut in 1/2-inch pieces
1/8 tsp. pepper	3 medium potatoes, cut in 1-inch cubes

Combine lamb and gravy mix in a 2–1/2-quart glass casserole. Microwave 5 minutes, uncovered. Stir in remaining ingredients. Cover. Microwave 20 minutes, stirring occasionally until meat and vegetables are tender. Makes 6 servings.

To obtain more juice from a lemon, microwave 30 seconds before squeezing.

PORK CHOP AND APPLE ROAST

When choosing the chops for this dish, pick thick ones which are as round as possible so they will fit the pan nicely.

6 thick pork chops
1/4 cup sugar
1 tsp. salt
1/2 tsp. pepper
1/4 tsp. cinnamon
1/4 tsp. nutmeg
2 tart apples, cored
1 large onion

Trim excess fat from the chops. Blend sugar, salt, pepper, cinnamon and nutmeg. Coat chops thoroughly. Stand them upright in a glass loaf pan. Cut apples into 7 slices and the onion into 5 slices. Place one of each between the chops, and the extra apple slices at each end. Cover tightly with plastic wrap. Microwave 14 to 15 minutes. Let rest 5 minutes before serving. Makes 6 servings.

SAVORY PORK CHOPS

Late getting home? Put this quick dish in your microwave oven, and dinner can be served in less than 20 minutes.

5 large or 6 medium pork chops
1 tbs. minced onion
1 tbs. Worcestershire sauce
1 can (10–3/4 ozs.) cream of mushroom soup, undiluted

Trim fat from chops. Arrange in an 8 x 12-inch baking dish in one layer, if possible. Sprinkle with onion and Worcestershire. Spread soup over top. Cover with waxed paper. Microwave about 18 minutes until tender. Makes 5 to 6 servings.

To heat rolls, microwave 10 to 15 seconds per roll. Frosted rolls heat faster than plain because of the higher sugar content.

SWEDISH HAM SLICES

Baked ham is elegant when prepared in the Scandinavian manner. An excellent choice for a buffet supper. If serving with rice, double the sauce ingredients and microwave one minute longer.

8 to 10 slices baked ham
1/2 cup dry white wine
1/2 cup whipping cream
1/2 tsp. curry powder
2 tbs. chili sauce

Early in the day, slice ham to desired thickness. Arrange ham slices in an 8 x 12-inch glass baking dish. Pour wine over ham. Cover with plastic and marinate. Mix cream, curry powder and chili sauce together. Cover and refrigerate. At serving time, pour off the wine. Spoon curry sauce over ham slices. Cover with waxed paper. Microwave 6 to 7 minutes until heated through. Serve extra sauce in a bowl. Makes 4 to 6 servings.

UPSIDE-DOWN HAM LOAF

Leftover ham won't be recognized in this delicious disguise.

2 tbs. butter
1/2 cup crushed pineapple
2 tbs. brown sugar
2 eggs, beaten
2 tbs. chopped onion
1/2 tsp. dry mustard
1/2 cup dried bread crumbs
1/2 cup pineapple juice
4 cups ground, cooked ham

Melt butter in a 9 x 5-inch glass loaf pan. Drain pineapple well, reserving juice. Spread pineapple over melted butter. Sprinkle with brown sugar. Mix the remaining ingredients together. Lightly pack into prepared loaf pan. Microwave 15 minutes, turning 1/4 turn every 3 minutes. Let rest a few minutes. Invert loaf onto serving platter. Makes 8 servings.

HAM RINGS

Serve with Mustard Sauce on page 38. If your family is small, freeze half for another meal. You'll be glad you did.

10 slices canned pineapple
1-1/2 lbs. ground ham ⎫
1/2 lb. ground pork ⎭ **or** 2 lbs. ground ham
2 eggs
1-1/2 cups soft bread crumbs
1 cup milk
1 tsp. horseradish sauce
salt and pepper to taste
1/2 cup white vinegar
1/2 cup brown sugar
1/2 cup pineapple juice
1 tsp. dry mustard

Drain pineapple, reserving the juice. Dry pineapple slices very well on paper toweling. Mix ham, pork, eggs, bread crumbs, milk, horseradish sauce, salt and pepper together well. Divide into 20 balls. Flatten into patties larger than pineapple slices. Place one pineapple slice on each of 10 patties. Top pineapple with the remaining ten patties. Seal the edges well. Poke a finger through the center to make a donut shape, and seal the inner edges. Place 6 ham rings in a 8 x 12-inch glass pan and the remainder into an 8-inch square glass pan. Mix remaining ingredients for sauce. Microwave 2 minutes. Pour over ham rings. Cover with waxed paper. Microwave 9 to 10 minutes for the larger pan, and 7 to 8 minutes for the smaller pan. Let rest a few minutes before serving. The pineapple gets so hot it will prevent the first pan of ham rings from cooling while the second pan is being cooked. Makes 10 servings.

SAUSAGE AND APPLE CASSEROLE

Here is a budget pleaser as well as taste teaser.

1 lb. link sausages
4 medium apples, pared, cored and thinly sliced
1-1/2 tbs. sugar

1/4 tsp. cinnamon
1 tbs. butter

Place sausages on four layers of paper towels and cover with another towel. Microwave 4 minutes. While sausages are cooking, arrange apple slices in a 9-inch Corningware casserole with cover. Sprinkle with sugar and cinnamon. Add butter. Cover. Microwave 4 minutes, stirring gently after 2 minutes. Arrange sausages on top. Microwave 1 minute more. Makes 4 servings.

Hot syrup on pancakes makes them taste even better. Syrup heats very quickly because of its high sugar content. Pour it into a glass pitcher. For 12 ounces (3/4 cup), microwave 30 to 45 seconds. Adjust timing for other quantities proportionately.

GRANDMA'S CORNED BEEF SPECIAL

If you are lucky enough to have one or two cups of leftover corned beef, use it In this recipe. The touch of dry mustard makes a sprightly difference.

1 pkg. (8 ozs.) noodles
1 can (12 ozs.) corned beef, crumbled
1/4 cup chopped onion
2 cups (8 ozs.) grated sharp cheddar cheese
1/2 tsp. dry mustard
salt and pepper to taste
1 tbs. butter or margarine
1/4 cup dried bread crumbs

Cook noodles conventionally in lightly salted water. Drain well. Mix beef, onion and cheese in a 1–1/2-quart casserole. Stir in noodles, mustard, salt and pepper. Put butter in a small dish and microwave 45 seconds to melt. Add crumbs. Sprinkle over mixture. Microwave 6 minutes until bubbly. Garnish with parsley if desired. Makes 6 servings.

POULTRY

Poultry cooked in a microwave oven is jucier and more delicately flavored than when cooked by other methods. Since chicken cooks rapidly, it may need to be browned first in a large frying pan or under a conventional broiler, or easiest of all, brush with paprika, soy sauce, diluted Kitchen Bouquet or Adolph's Seasoning for a browned appearance.

When arranging cut-up poultry in your oven, be sure the larger, thicker pieces are on the outside and the smaller pieces in the middle. A cover of waxed paper or paper toweling will prevent spattering.

Whole turkeys can be cooked in a microwave oven, and because of their long cooking time they will brown beautifully. Just be sure to choose one that is compact and of a size that can be rotated easily in your oven. Read your manual instructions carefully for more detailed information. Lay a paper towel over turkey to prevent spatters.

Stuffing a turkey or chicken will not increase the cooking time in a microwave oven as it does in a conventional oven.

TURKEY BREAST WITH STUFFING

Nice when a small family suddenly gets hungry for turkey and stuffing.

3 to 4 lb. turkey breast half
1 tbs. salad oil
1 tbs. Kitchen Bouquet
1/2 cup butter
1 cup chopped celery

1 medium onion, chopped
1/4 cup minced parsley
1 pkg. (8 ozs.) stuffing mix
1 cup chicken broth

Rinse and dry turkey breast. Trim away excess fat and skin. Lightly salt cut side only. Place skin side up in a casserole or glass baking dish. Combine oil and Kitchen Bouquet. Brush over turkey. Microwave 10 minutes. Remove turkey to a plate. Set aside. Place butter, celery, onion and parsley in dish with drippings. Tightly cover with plastic wrap. Microwave 5 minutes. Stir. Add stuffing mix and broth. Stir until well mixed. Lay breast on top of stuffing. Push stuffing under breast. Cover with waxed paper. Microwave 17 to 20 minutes depending on size of turkey breast. Turn pan halfway through the cooking time. Allow to stand a few minutes before carving. Makes 4 to 6 servings.

CHICKEN IN A BAG

Paper bags are great in microwave ovens. The microwaves pass right through the bag, which eliminates all mess from spattering.

3 tbs. catsup
2 tbs. Worcestershire sauce
2 tbs. vinegar
1 tbs. lemon juice
2 tbs. butter

3 tbs. brown sugar
1 tsp salt
1 tsp. dry mustard
1 tsp. paprika
2-1/2 to 3 lb. chicken parts

Mix all ingredients except chicken in a large glass baking dish or Corningware pan. Microwave 2 minutes, stirring often. Dip chicken into sauce and place in a clean brown bag. Fold end over and slip in a second bag. Place on a large platter. Microwave 18 to 21 minutes (7 minutes per pound). Let rest a few minutes before serving. Makes 4 to 6 servings.

CHICKEN BOLA GAI

The soy sauce imparts a beautiful color as well as delicious flavor, making browning unnecessary.

1/3 cup all-purpose flour
1 tsp. salt
1/2 tsp. celery salt
1/2 tsp. nutmeg
1/4 tsp. garlic salt
6 chicken breast halves
1/4 cup butter
1 can (15-1/2 ozs.) pineapple chunks
1/2 cup soy sauce
2 tbs. sugar
2 tsp. cornstarch
1/4 cup water
3 cups cooked rice

Mix together flour, salt, celery salt and nutmeg. Skin chicken breasts and dip into mixture. Melt butter in an 8 x 12-inch glass baking dish. Microwave 45 seconds. Turn chicken over in the butter to coat both sides. Begin cooking with meaty side down. Drain pineapple, reserving juice. Combine juice with soy sauce and sugar. Pour over chicken. Cover with plastic wrap. Microwave 5 minutes. Turn chicken over. Baste. Microwave 5 minutes, covered. Baste. Add pineapple. Microwave 5 minutes until chicken is tender. Combine cornstarch with water. Remove chicken to a warm platter. Add cornstarch mixture to pineapple and pan drippings. Microwave 2 minutes until thick and bubbly. Serve sauce over chicken and rice. Makes 6 servings.

CHICKEN CURRY

This tastiest of curries is also the easiest, and the chicken cuts like butter.

6 chicken breast halves
salt
paprika
2 tbs. butter
2 to 3 tsp. curry powder
1 apple, chopped fine
1 small onion, minced
1 can (10–3/4 ozs.) cream of mushroom soup, undiluted
1/2 cup dry white wine
cooked rice
condiments: chopped green onion, chopped salted peanuts,
coconut, raisins, chutney

Skin and bone breasts. Wash and dry well. Arrange on an 8 x 12-inch glass baking dish. Salt lightly and dust with paprika. Measure butter into a small bowl.

Microwave 45 seconds to melt. Add curry, apple and onion. Stir. Cover. Microwave 1-1/2 minutes until onion is limp. Stir in soup and wine. Pour over chicken. Microwave 12 to 14 minutes. Serve chicken on beds of rice. Spoon sauce and your favorite condiments over the top. Makes 6 servings.

CALIFORNIA CHICKEN

This simply prepared dish is unbelievably flavorful.

2-1/2 to 3 lb. frying chicken
salt
1 tsp. thyme
1 clove garlic, minced
8 tbs. (1/4 lb.) butter, softened
1 medium zucchini, sliced thin
4 to 6 artichoke hearts
6 to 8 small onions or leeks
2 to 3 carrots, cut up
1 tbs. salad oil

Wash chicken and pat dry. Salt the cavity. Carefully work your fingers in between the meat and the skin to loosen. Blend thyme, garlic and 6 tablespoons butter together. Chill in the refrigerator or freezer while preparing the vegetables. Then work the butter mixture under the skin of the chicken, starting with the breasts.

Work it around the legs. Be very careful not to tear the skin. Heat remaining 2 tablespoons butter and the oil in an electric skillet or on top of the range. Brown chicken well on all sides. Remove to a 3-quart casserole. Cover and microwave 10 minutes. Meanwhile, toss the vegetables in the butter and oil remaining in the skillet. Sprinkle with salt. Add, along with the drippings, to the chicken. Cover tightly. Microwave 12 minutes until the chicken is tender. Makes 4 to 6 servings.

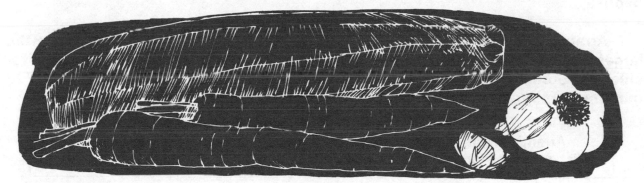

SAUCY CHICKEN

Chicken the easy way, with enough gravy for noodles or rice.

2-1/2 to 3 lb. frying chicken, cut up
1 can (10-3/4 ozs.) golden mushroom soup, undiluted
1 can (4 ozs.) mushrooms, drained
1 tsp. salt
paprika

Arrange chicken skin side up in an 8 x 12-inch glass baking dish. Place the largest pieces toward the outside. Mix soup, mushrooms and salt. Spoon over chicken. Sprinkle with paprika. Cover with waxed paper. Microwave 25 to 28 minutes, turning dish occasionally, until chicken is done. Makes 4 to 5 servings.

Arrange fresh vegetables such as broccoli and cauliflower so that stem which takes the longest to cook is toward the outside of the dish.

GLAZED DRUMSTRICKS

Serve this and you will evoke the South Seas.

8 plump chicken legs, skin removed
1/2 cup apricot-pineapple preserves
1 tsp. cornstarch
1/2 tsp. salt
1 tbs. teriyaki sauce.

Arrange chicken, meat side down, in a glass baking dish. Mix remaining ingredients. Brush over chicken. Cover with waxed paper. Microwave 10 to 15 minutes (7 minutes per pound), turning chicken half way through the cooking time, basting several times. Makes 4 servings.

CHICKEN ON A BLANKET

Use leftover chicken or turkey, or cook six meaty chicken breast halves for this pleasingly flavored dish.

1 pkg. (10 ozs.) frozen spinach, defrosted
1 pkg. (8 ozs.) cream cheese
1 cup milk
1 cup (4 ozs.) shredded Monterey Jack cheese
1/2 tsp. salt
1/4 tsp. garlic salt
1/2 cup Parmesan cheese
2 cups cooked cubed chicken or turkey
1/4 cup crushed cereal (Special K, cornflakes or Wheaties)

To defrost spinach, see page 4. Squeeze dry or drain well. Spread spinach in a 9-inch Corningware casserole or 8-inch glass pan. To make sauce, blend cream cheese, milk, Monterey Jack cheese, salt, garlic salt and 1/4 cup Parmesan cheese together in a small glass bowl. Microwave 2 minutes, stirring often. Spread half the sauce over spinach. Sprinkle chicken over sauce, and top with remaining sauce. Sprinkle remaining 1/4 cup Parmesan cheese and the cereal over top. Microwave 6 minutes until bubbly. For added color, place under conventional broiler until lightly browned. Makes 6 servings.

To soften cream cheese, place it in a glass bowl or on a paper plate. Microwave 5 seconds, rest 10 seconds. Repeat one or two more times until very soft. Stir, if necessary, to help equalize the temperature. Do not overcook as the edges will melt.

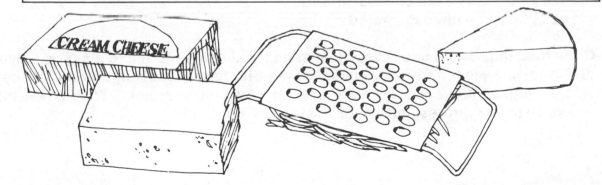

CHICKEN OLE

A favorite which must be refrigerated several hours to blend flavors.

2 cups cooked chicken or turkey
1 can (10-3/4 ozs.) cream of celery or mushroom soup, undiluted
1 cup (1/2 pt.) sour cream
1/2 cup milk
1/2 cup green chile salsa
6 corn tortillas, torn into small pieces
1 onion, chopped
1 cup (4 ozs.) Monterey Jack cheese, grated
1 cup (4 ozs.) Cheddar cheese, grated

Cube chicken. Blend soup, sour cream and chile salsa to make a sauce. Layer half of the tortilla pieces in a 1-1/2-quart casserole. Layer chicken, onions, cheese and sauce. Repeat. Cover. Refrigerate several hours or overnight. With cover on, microwave 10 to 12 minutes, until bubbly. Makes 4 servings.

CORNY CHICKEN

A simple one-dish meal, also good made with ham or tuna.

1 pkg. (10 ozs.) frozen chopped broccoli or broccoli cuts
1 can (8 ozs.) cream-style corn
1 can (8 ozs.) whole kernel corn, drained
1 can (10–3/4 ozs.) cream of chicken soup, undiluted
2 cups cooked cubed chicken or turkey
2 tbs. butter or margarine
1 cup crushed cheese or chicken flavored crackers

Defrost broccoli following directions on page 4. Drain accumulated moisture. Combine broccoli, both types of corn, soup and chicken in a 2-quart casserole or an 8 x 12-inch glass pan. Place butter in a small bowl and microwave 45 seconds to melt. Add cracker crumbs and sprinkle over chicken mixture. Microwave 8 to 10 minutes, uncovered, until bubbly. Makes 6 to 8 servings.

SEAFOOD

Fresh or frozen seafood is ideally cooked in a microwave oven. It must be cooked only until it flakes, rested briefly and served. Overcooking toughens it and destroys its delicate flavor. Unlike meats and casseroles, it does not reheat well.

Fish may be cooked whole, as fillets or as steaks. When cooking fillets tuck under or overlap the very thin, tapering edges so they will be about the same thickness and cook evenly. Fresh, whole fish is cooked one minute per pound on each side. Steaks and fillets prepared with additional ingredients should be microwaved four to five minutes per pound. Sole, turbot, perch, white fish, halibut and snapper can be interchanged in all recipes in this book.

Natural shells make perfect containers for cooking and serving seafood dishes. To keep them balanced in the oven, it helps to set them on a small terry towel. Arrange them in a circle with none in the center.

CRABMEAT IN SHELLS

Just right for an elegant meal, especially when crab is in season.

1 cup (1/4 lb. fresh or 1 small can) crabmeat
2 tsp. lemon juice
1/2 lb. mushrooms, washed and sliced
6 tbs. butter
2 tbs. all-purpose flour
1/2 ts. salt
1/8 tsp. white pepper
1 cup milk
2 egg yolks
2 tbs. sherry
1/2 cup dried bread crumbs
parsley, lemon slices

Clean and flake crab. Sprinkle with lemon juice and set aside. Put 4 table-spoons butter and the mushrooms in a glass bowl or casserole. Cover with lid or plastic wrap. Microwave 2 minutes. Remove mushrooms. Add flour and seasonings to the drippings. Microwave 30 seconds. Add milk and egg yolks. Stir well. (A wire whisk helps.) Microwave 2-1/2 minutes, stirring often, until thickened. Gently stir sherry, mushrooms and crab into sauce. Spoon into 4 buttered baking shells or ramekins. Melt remaining 2 tablespoons butter. Stir in crumbs. Sprinkle over crab mixture. Microwave 6 to 7 minutes until bubbly. If made ahead and refrigerated, add 1 to 2 minutes to the cooking time. Garnish with lemon slices and parsley. Makes 4 servings.

Note: The baking shells are more stable if placed on a towel on a plate.

CURRIED SHRIMP

While the rice cooks conventionally, prepare sauce to spoon over it.

1/4 cup butter	1 cup milk
1/2 to 1 tsp. curry powder	1/4 cup catsup
1/2 tsp. salt	1/4 cup sherry
dash paprika	1–1/2 cups (1/2 lb.) shrimp
1/4 cup all-purpose flour	4 cups cooked rice

In a 1-quart casserole, melt butter for 30 seconds. Stir in curry, salt, paprika and flour. Add milk. Stir until blended. Microwave 3–1/2 minues, stirring frequently. Add catsup and sherry. Gently stir in shrimp. Just before serving, microwave 2 minutes until hot and bubbly. Serve on fluffy rice. Garnish with parsley. Makes 4 servings.

To heat water microwave 1 minute on high (100%) power per cup for hot water, 2 to 3 minutes for boiling water.

SHRIMP AND WILD RICE

Save this for a very special occasion—then splurge delightfully.

1 cup wild rice
1 lb. shrimp
2 tbs. lemon juice
1/2 cup onion
1/4 cup butter
1 cup sliced mushrooms
1 can (10-3/4 ozs.) tomato soup, undiluted
1/2 cup light cream
1/4 cup sherry

Cook wild rice conventionally according to package directions. Marinate shrimp in lemon juice. Meanwhile, mix remaining ingredients in a 2-1/2-quart casserole. Add rice and shrimp, including lemon juice. Cover. Microwave 10 minutes. Allow to rest before serving. Leftovers reheat well. Makes 8 to 10 servings.

CRUMB COATED FILLETS

Paprika gives the fish a delightful color. Any fish fillets may be used, but perch is particularly nice. Allow four minutes per pound when cooking fillets and thickly cut steaks.

1–1/4 lb. fish fillets
1/2 cup corn bread stuffing mix
1/4 cup Parmesan cheese

1 tsp. thyme
1/2 tsp. paprika
2 tbs. butter or margarine

Rinse and dry the fillets. Combine stuffing mix, cheese, thyme and paprika in blender container. Cover and blend 15 seconds to crush (or finely crush stuffing mix with a rolling pin and then mix it with cheese and seasonings). Place butter in an 8 x 12-inch glass pan. Microwave 45 seconds to melt. Dip fillets in melted butter, then in crumb mixture. Arrange in the same glass pan. Cover with waxed paper. Microwave 5 to 6 minutes until fish flakes. Do not overcook. Allow to stand a few minutes, covered, before serving. Makes 6 servings.

MICROWAVE'S MARVELOUS FISH

Prepare fish in the microwave oven just once and you'll never cook it any other way. This is a perfect recipe for cooking any kind of fish fillet.

1 lb. fish fillets
4 tbs. butter or margarine
1 tbs. chopped fresh parsley
2 tbs. fresh lemon juice
1/2 tsp. salt
dash pepper

Thaw fish if frozen. Measure butter into a microwave-safe dish big enough to hold the fish in a single layer. Microwave at 50% power for 2 minutes or until melted. Blend 1 tablespoon of the parsley with melted butter. Dip each fillet in the parsley-butter sauce coating both sides. Arrange fillets with thick sides toward the outside of the dish. Pour lemon juice evenly over fillets. Sprinkle with salt and pepper and remaining 1 tablespoon parsley. Cover tightly with plastic wrap. Microwave at 100% power 6 to 8 minutes or until fish flakes easily with a fork. Let rest covered 4 minutes before serving. Makes 2 to 3 servings.

STUFFED SOLE SURPRISES

Baby shrimp flavored with dill makes the surprise filling.

1 lb. sole fillets
1/4 lb. baby shrimp
1/4 cup fine dried bread crumbs
1/2 tsp. fines herbes
1/2 tsp. onion salt
1/4 tsp. dill weed
3 tbs. mayonnaise
1/4 cup grated Parmesan cheese
salt
Shrimp Sauce, page 101

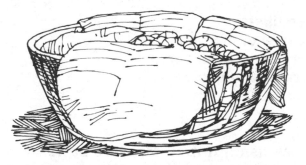

Rinse and dry fillets. Rinse shrimp, and mix with remaining ingredients. Butter four 6-ounce Pyrex custard cups (or suitable coffee cups). Arrange fillets in them to cover the bottom and sides, allowing excess to extend over rim of cups. Lightly spoon shrimp filling into cups. Then bring the excess sole over the shrimp, enclosing it. Place in the oven in a circle. Cover loosely with plastic wrap or waxed paper. Microwave 7 minutes. Rest 1 minute. Pour off excess moisture, then turn out onto serving plates. Serve with Shrimp Sauce. Makes 4 servings.

SHRIMP SAUCE

1 can (10-3/4 ozs.) cream of shrimp soup, undiluted
2 tbs. sherry
1 tbs. snipped chives

Mix together in a suitable small pitcher. Microwave 2 minutes. Stir and serve.

Note: If desired, shrimp may be layered between filets in glass baking dish. Cover and cook as directed.

SALMON PUFF

Best when assembled early in the day, then microwave 8 minutes and dinner is ready.

1 can (1 lb.) pink or red salmon
2 cups seasoned croutons
2 cups (8 ozs.) grated cheddar cheese
4 eggs
1–1/2 cups milk
1/2 tsp. Worcestershire sauce
1/2 tsp. dry mustard
1 tsp. salt

Drain and flake salmon. Place 1 cup croutons in a 2-quart casserole. Sprinkle 1 cup salmon and 1 cup cheese over croutons. Repeat layers. Beat eggs. Blend in remaining ingredients. Pour over the layers. Sprinkle with paprika, if desired. Microwave 6 minutes, until just set, if cooked immediately; or 8 minutes if mixture has been refrigerated. Makes 6 servings.

DISNEYLAND TUNABURGERS

Good with raw carrot sticks, Poached Pears (page 132) and sugar cookies.

1 can (6-1/2 ozs.) tuna
1 tbs. chopped onion
1/4 cup chopped celery
1 tsp. lemon juice
1/4 cup mayonnaise

4 hamburger buns
2 tbs. catsup
sweet pickle slices
4 slices processed cheese

Mix together tuna, onion, celery, lemon juice and 2 tablespoons mayonnaise. Slice buns into three layers. Mix remaining mayonnaise with catusp. Spread on the bottom bun slice. Cover with pickle slices and a slice of cheese. Put middle bun slice on top. Spread tuna mixture on middle slice. Replace bun top. Place sandwiches on paper towels, with another paper towel on top. Microwave 1–1/2 minutes until hot. Makes 4.

VEGETABLES

You may have a crockery pot you enjoy using to slowly cook less tender cuts of meat, but for cooking vegetables, a microwave oven is unsurpassed. Not only is the color superior, but the nutrient value is the highest. Because little water is added, texture and fresh-picked flavor are retained.

Squash, pumpkin, eggplant and potatoes are cooked with their skins on, acting as a tight wrap. Remember to pierce in several places before cooking to allow steam to escape. Beets are also cooked with their skins on, in just eight minutes instead of the usual forty.

Frozen vegetables are best cooked in a covered casserole with no additional water. Stir to separate and distribute heat evenly. They can be thawed right in the carton. Cut an X in the top for the steam to escape.

Microwave canned vegetables two minutes per cup. Heat in their serving dish with or without liquid.

Always add seasonings after heating to prevent the salt from drying out the vegetables.

ARTICHOKES

So fast and easy you'll want to serve this favorite vegetable often.

2 medium artichokes (about 3-1/2 inches in diameter)
1 lemon

Wash artichokes. Cut stem and prickly tips from each. Trim tips of leaves to remove thorns. Rub cut edges with lemon to prevent browning. Run under water and tightly wrap, individually, in plastic wrap. Microwave 6 to 7 minutes. Remove wrap and turn upside down to drain. Spread leaves and remove fuzzy choke from the center, using a spoon. Fill the well with Hollandaise Sauce, page 35, mayonnaise or lemon butter. Makes 2 servings, or, if preferred, cut in half for 4 servings.

Microwave timing for other quantities:
1 artichoke	4 to 4-1/2 minutes
3 artichokes	8 to 9 minutes
4 artichokes	10 to 11 minutes

RUSSIAN BEETS

Grated beets are enhanced by a tangy sour cream sauce.

4 medium beets, cooked*
1 tbs. butter
1 tbs. all-purpose flour
1 tbs. sugar
1 tbs. white vinegar
1/4 tsp. salt
1/4 cup sour cream

Grate cooked beets. Melt butter in a 1-quart casserole. Stir in flour. Add sugar, vinegar and salt. Stir well, then add grated beets. Microwave 2 minutes. Add sour cream. Microwave 1/2 to 1 minutes, just to heat through. Makes 5 to 6 servings.

*To cook, place four trimmed beets in a large casserole with lid. Add 1/2 cup water. Cover. Microwave 10 minutes per pound, until tender. Drain and peel.

BROCCOLI

Broccoli cooked in a microwave oven retains its beautiful bright green color.

1 lb. broccoli
1/4 cup water

Soak broccoli heads in salted water for ten minutes to remove any foreign matter. Split stems for uniform size. Arrange in a large casserole with cover, placing stems toward the outside. Add water. Cover. Microwave 6 to 7 minutes, until stems are tender. Serve with lemon butter or any of the following sauces: Hollandaise, page 36; Mornay, page 34; Mustard, page 39; or Cheese, page 38.

Note: If broccoli is chopped up, cooking time will be slightly shorter.

> If cooking fresh vegetables ahead, undercook by two minutes. Remove from oven and keep covered. The retained heat will continue to cook the vegetables.

CAULIFLOWER

Soak the cauliflower in salted water before preparing. This will force out any creepy crawlers lurking under the surface.

1 medium cauliflower
2 tbs. water

Rinse the cauliflower and cut off any dark age spots. If cooking as flowerets, separate them. Place in a large casserole with lid. Add water. Cover. Microwave 10 minutes for whole, or 8 minutes for flowerets. Drain. Season to taste. Delicious with buttered bread crumbs, Cheese Sauce, page 38 or Mornay Sauce, page 37. Makes 5 to 6 servings.

CAULIFLOWER CURRY

Extraordinary blending of flavors puts this cauliflower in a special class.

1 large cauliflower
2 tbs. water
1 can (10–3/4 ozs.) cream of chicken soup, undiluted
1 cup (4 ozs.) grated cheddar cheese
1/3 cup mayonnaise
1/2 to 1 tsp. curry powder
2 tbs. butter, melted
1/4 cup dry bread crumbs

Break cauliflower into flowerets. Place in a 1–1/2-quart casserole. Add water. Cover. Microwave 7 minutes. Drain in colander. In same casserole, mix soup, cheese, mayonnaise and curry powder. Gently fold in cauliflower. Microwave butter 1 minute. Add crumbs. Sprinkle over cauliflower. Microwave 3 minutes, uncovered. Makes 6 to 8 servings.

SCALLOPED CHERRY TOMATOES

When your garden is brimming over with cherry tomatoes, scallop them.

1/4 cup chopped onion	pinch oregano
1 full basket cherry tomatoes	1/2 tsp. sugar
1 tsp. salt	1 tbs. butter or margarine
1/8 tsp. pepper	1/4 cup bread crumbs
1/2 tsp. thyme	2 tsp. chopped parsley

Put onion in a small bowl. Add 1 tablespoon water. Cover. Microwave 2-1/2 minutes. Put washed tomatoes in a 1-quart casserole. Add onion, salt, pepper, thyme, oregano and sugar. Mix well. Place butter in a small dish and microwave 30 seconds until melted. Add crumbs and parsley. Sprinkle over tomatoes. Cover. Microwave 4 minutes. If not served immediately, reheat 1-1/2 minutes until hot. Makes 4 servings.

CORN ON THE COB

This method is much easier than cooking in the husks, especially if young children are to handle the corn.

4 medium ears of corn
butter
salt and pepper to taste

Remove all husks and clean off the silk. Run under water. Do not dry, but immediately wrap in waxed paper or plastic wrap. Leave the ends open. Place in the oven. Microwave 6 to 8 minutes, depending on size. Remove. Wait one minute, then slip out of the wrapping. Serve with butter, salt and pepper.

Note: If cooking 6 ears or more, it is easier to use a large casserole with cover or a baking dish with plastic wrap. Add two tablespoons water and cover tightly. Microwave 8 to 9 minutes.

CORN SOUFFLE

Delightful on a cold winter evening.

1 egg
4 whole saltines, broken
1 can (14 ozs.) cream style corn
salt and pepper to taste

Beat egg in a small casserole. Add the remaining ingredients and stir. Microwave 5 minutes, stirring often, just until set. Let rest a few minutes before serving. Makes 4 servings.

CORN STUFFED TOMATOES

Another party dish with eye appeal. If only making four, use half a package of corn, and microwave slightly less time.

6 medium tomatoes
salt
1 pkg. (10 ozs.) frozen cut corn, defrosted
2 tbs. butter
1/4 cup chopped green onion

1/2 tsp. salt
1/8 tsp. pepper
2 tbs. bread crumbs
1/4 cup Parmesan cheese

Cut off tops of tomatoes and scoop out the pulp. This is easy with a melon baller or grapefruit knife. Salt the insides of the shells, then turn over to drain. Put remaining ingredients in a small bowl. Microwave two minutes, stirring after one minute. Fill tomatoes. Place on a serving dish. Microwave 4 to 5 minutes until warm. If made ahead and refrigerated, add one minute to the final microwave time. Makes 6 servings.

BAKED POTATOES

Many people feel that a microwave oven justifies itself for this job alone.

Pick uniform potatoes of MEDIUM size (6 to 8 ozs. each*). Scrub well and prick several times with a fork. On a paper towel or plate, arrange potatoes in a circle with none in the center, and one inch of space between each potato. Microwave as follows:

1 potato	3-1/2 to 4 minutes
2 potatoes	6-1/2 to 7 minutes
3 potatoes	8-1/2 to 9 minutes
4 potatoes	10 to 11 minutes
5 potatoes	13 to 14 minutes
6 potatoes	15 to 16 minutes
7 potatoes	18 to 19 minutes
8 potatoes	21 to 22 minutes

*If potatoes are larger, it will take a longer time. Don't forget that potatoes continue to cook after they are removed from the oven, so do not overcook.

STUFFED BAKED POTATOES

Pretty to look at, good to taste, but best of all, these can be made ahead and refrigerated or frozen.

4 potatoes, scrubbed
4 tbs. butter or margarine
1/2 cup milk, slightly warmed (microwave 30 seconds)
salt and pepper to taste
paprika, chopped chives, or crumbled bacon to garnish

Bake potatoes as directed on page 115. Let rest five minutes, uncovered, then cut a slice off the upper third. Carefully scoop out potato into a mixing bowl. Save the shells. Mash with a masher or electric mixer. Add butter and milk. Season to taste with salt and pepper. Spoon back into the potato shells. Garnish as desired. Microwave 3 minutes (5 minutes if refrigerated, 15 minutes if frozen) until hot. Makes 4 servings.

SURPRISE BAKED POTATOES

A delicious and unusual variation of everyone's favorite.

4 medium (6 to 8 ozs. each) potatoes, pared
2 medium mild onions
1/4 cup softened butter
paprika

Cut each potato crosswise into 4 slices and each onion into 6 slices. Butter each potato slice. Reassemble, sandwiching onion slices between potato slices. Secure with toothpicks. Arrange in a circle on a plate or pie dish. Sprinkle with paprika. Cover tightly with plastic wrap. Microwave 16 to 18 minutes until done. If desired, brown under broiler. To serve, garnish with chopped parsley. Makes 4 servings.

> To soften butter, unwrap and lay on a plate. Microwave 5 seconds on medium (50%) power, then rest 15 seconds. Microwave another 5 seconds and rest 15 seconds. Microwave 5 seconds more, if needed.

GERMAN POTATO SALAD

No longer a last minute dish, now it can be made ahead and easily reheated. Just cover and microwave 1 to 2 minutes.

8 medium potatoes
1/2 cup chopped celery
4 hard-cooked eggs
1/2 cup chopped onion
salt and pepper to taste

6 slices bacon
1/4 cup sugar
1/4 cup all-purpose flour
1/3 cup vinegar
1-1/2 cups milk

Bake potatoes according to directions on page 115. Peel and dice potatoes into a large casserole. Add celery, eggs, onion, salt and pepper. Set aside. Dice bacon into a small bowl. Microwave 5 minutes. Mix together sugar and flour. Add this to bacon and drippings, then add vinegar and milk. Microwave 4 to 5 minutes, stirring once or twice, until thickened. Pour over potatoes. Serve warm. Makes 6 to 8 servings.

PINEAPPLE YAM BOATS

Nice not only at Thanksgiving, but any time turkey or ham is on the menu. If prepared ahead and refrigerated, add 1 minute to the final heating time.

4 medium (7 to 8 ozs. each) yams or sweet potatoes
2 tbs. butter or margarine
2 tbs. brown sugar
2 tsp. grated lemon rind
1/4 tsp. ground ginger
1/4 tsp. salt
1 cup crushed pineapple

Scrub yams and prick several times with a fork. Place on a paper towel in the microwave oven, arranging in a circle. Microwave 15 minutes until tender, turning over halfway through the cooking time. Cool slightly. Cut off a thin slice of the top from each. Carefully scoop out the insides, reserving the shells. Add the seasonings to the yams and mash. Drain pineapple, adding two tablespoons of the juice to the yams. Carefully fold in the pineapple. Fill the shells with mixture. Place in a circle on a serving plate. Microwave 3 minutes until heated through. Makes 4 servings.

PEACH YAM BOATS

Substitute diced peaches for the pineapple, and use 2 tablespoons brandy instead of pineapple juice.

BANANA SQUASH

Try this instead of the more common acorn squash. Its bright orange color adds a festive touch to any dinner plate.

1 large piece banana squash
butter
salt, pepper, nutmeg

Wash the squash. Cover the cut side tightly with plastic wrap. Place in the microwave oven with the rind down. Microwave about 8 minutes per pound until soft enough to scrape into a serving bowl. Mash with a fork. Add remaining ingredients to taste. Just before serving, microwave 2 to 3 minutes. Makes 4 servings.

> Butter softens, melts, and bubbles faster than margarine. Oil heats very slowly. When a recipe calls for heating a large quantity of oil, use your conventional range.

SPAGHETTI SQUASH

Serve with easy Spaghetti Sauce on page 56 for a tasty, low-calorie version of a favorite. It's also good with butter, salt, pepper and Parmesan cheese.

2 to 3 lb. spaghetti squash

Wash. Pierce with a fork or make several slits with a knife. Place on a folded paper towel or paper plate. Microwave about 6 minutes per pound, turning once or twice. If it starts to hiss before time is up, poke again with a fork. Cool ten minutes, then cut in half lengthwise. Scoop out the flesh. This type of squash separates into long shreds much like spaghetti, hence the name, and has a crunchy al dente texture. Serve with spaghetti sauce. It reheats well and freezes beautifully. Makes 6 to 8 servings.

WINTER SQUASH, BAKED WHOLE

No longer is it necessary to find a strong man to cut open winter squash. Bake it whole, then slip the knife through with ease.

1 whole acorn or butternut squash

Wash the squash and poke holes with a fork to allow steam to escape. Place on a paper plate. Microwave 5 to 6 minutes per pound. Turn once or twice while it is cooking. Cut open. Clean out the seeds and season with any of the following: butter, brown sugar, honey, cinnamon, cooked fruit such as apples or cranberries, sausage, maple syrup, nutmeg or dill. Makes 4 to 8 servings.

ZUCCHINI PUDDING

This tempting dish will make you happy your zucchini plant is prolific.

1 medium or 3 very small zucchini, unpeeled
1 tbs. butter or margarine
1/2 medium onion, chopped
1 clove garlic, crushed
1/4 cup dry bread crumbs
1/4 tsp. each thyme and marjoram
1/2 tsp. salt
ground pepper
2 eggs, beaten

Grate zucchini. In a 1-quart casserole, melt butter. Add onion and garlic. Microwave 2 minutes. Add zucchini. Microwave 3 minutes. Add remaining ingredients. Mix well. Microwave 4-1/2 minutes, stirring often, just until set. Rest for a few minutes before serving. Makes 4 servings.

STUFFED ZUCCHINI

This Mexican inspired recipe looks complicated but really isn't. The flavorful combination is nice for company, especially at Christmastime. Begin the sauce first as it must be cooked conventionally on the range in order for it to be reduced.

5 medium (5-inch long) zucchini
1 pkg. (10 ozs.) frozen corn, defrosted
2 eggs

1/4 tsp. salt
1/2 lb. Cheddar cheese, grated
Herbed Tomato Sauce, next page

Wash zucchini and arrange in a 7- x 11-inch baking dish. Prick several times with a fork. Microwave on high power (100%) for 5 minutes. Cut in half. Scoop out seeds. Return to baking dish. In blender or food processor mix remaining ingredients except cheese and sauce, blending just until you have a coarse puree. Add 3/4 of the cheese to puree. Mix until just combined. Fill zucchini with mixture. Microwave on high 3 to 4 minutes until zucchini is barely tender. Sprinkle with remaining cheese. Microwave on medium-low (30%) power for 1 to 2 minutes until cheese has melted. Serve with Herbed Tomato Sauce. Makes 5 servings.

HERBED TOMATO SAUCE

3 tbs. oil
1/3 cup chopped onion
1 can (1 lb.) solid pack tomatoes, drained
2 small cloves garlic, crushed
1/2 tsp. salt
1/3 cup cilantro (Chinese, Italian or flat parsley) or parsley

    Heat oil to medium temperature in skillet on top of stove. Add onions, tomatoes, garlic and salt. Bring mixture to a boil. Reduce heat to low and cook until reduced by half, about 20 minutes. Stir in cilantro or parsley. Serve over zucchini. Leftover sauce is marvelous on omelets, fish, and other vegetables.

FRUITS

As with other foods that are successfully cooked in a microwave oven, fruits retain their flavor, color, texture, appearance and shape beautifully. Because they are high in sugar content, their cooking time is short. Cook them in a pretty dish and they are ready to be served.

To retain the shape of fruits such as apple slices, sugar is added before cooking. When a sauce consistency is desired, as for applesauce, sugar is added after cooking. It may be necessary to adjust the amount of sugar needed due to the variance in the tartness of some fruits.

When fruit is to be cut before cooking, make the pieces as uniform as possible for more even cooking.

Microwave chilled or frozen fruit to bring it to room temperature or to reheat, if it is to be served warm.

BAKED APPLE SLICES

Use tart, firm apples such as Granny Smith or Newtown Pippins because they retain their shape and texture. Serve as dessert or for breakfast.

1/2 cup pineapple juice
2 tbs. brown sugar
2 tbs. honey
1/4 cup dark or light raisins
4 large cooking apples
1/2 cup chopped nuts (optional)

Mix pineapple juice, brown sugar, honey and raisins in a 1-1/2-quart casserole. Microwave 1-1/2 minutes. Peel, core and thinly slice apples. Add to juice mixture. Add nuts. Cover. Microwave 8 minutes. Serve warm or well chilled. Makes 4 to 6 servings.

SPICY BAKED BANANAS

When bananas are at their best, remember this good tasting dessert.

6 firm ripe bananas
1/4 cup butter
2 tbs. lemon juice
1/4 tsp. ginger
1/8 tsp. clovers
1/2 tsp. cinnamon
1 tbs. sugar

Melt butter in an 8 x 12-inch glass baking dish. Microwave 45 seconds. Arrange peeled bananas in dish, rolling them in the melted butter. Sprinkle with lemon juice. Combine remaining ingredients. Sprinkle over bananas. Microwave 4 to 5 minutes until soft but not mushy. Makes 6 servings.

POACHED PEARS WITH RASPBERRY SAUCE

Easy, elegant, and not rich, this is perfect for any occasion.

2 cups pineapple juice
2 cups water
2 cups sugar

4 to 6 firm ripe pears
1 box frozen raspberries, thawed
1 cup vanilla ice cream

In a large casserole deep enough to accommodate whole pears, mix pineapple juice, water and sugar. Microwave 12 minutes until boiling, stirring a few times. Meanwhile peel the pears. Core each one by removing the seeds from the bottom (do not go all the way through) with a melon baller or teaspoon, leaving the pear whole and the stem intact. Set pears in syrup. Put a small plate or saucer over pears to keep them submerged in the syrup. Cover. Microwave 1-1/2 minutes, then allow to cool in syrup. Refrigerate until ready to use. Press raspberries through a sieve to remove seeds. Slightly soften ice cream by stirring. Stand chilled pears in individual dessert dishes. Spoon softened ice cream over the pears and top with raspberry sauce. Makes 4 to 6 servings.

RHUBARB BLUSH

It's simple to microwave this tasty springtime favorite.

3/4 lb. rhubarb (6 to 7 stalks)
2 tbs. water
2 tbs. sugar
1/2 pkg. (3 ozs.) raspberry gelatin

Wash rhubarb. Cut into small pieces. You should have about two cups. Put into a 1-1/2-quart casserole with water. Cover. Microwave 4 minutes, stirring once. Add sugar and gelatin. Stir well. Microwave 1 minute longer. Cool covered. Makes 4 servings.

A slice of pie a la mode (topped with ice cream) can be microwaved 30 to 45 seconds on high (100%) power to heat the pie without melting the ice cream.

FRUIT IN WINE AND HONEY

A satisfying dessert after a heavy meal.

1 cup honey
3/4 cup cider vinegar
10 whole cloves
1 stick cinnamon
3/4 cup port or muscatel wine
6 cups (two #2–1/2 cans) fruit, well drained

Combine honey, vinegar and spices in a glass bowl or casserole. Microwave 2 minutes. Add wine and fruit. Microwave 5 minutes. Cool. Store in refrigerator. Makes 6 servings.

ENGLISH PLUM PUDDING

At least six generations old, this traditional pudding once took 4 to 6 hours to steam. Now I cook it in the microwave oven in about 12 minutes!

1 lb. raisins
1/2 lb. ground suet (see your butcher)*
4 cups all-purpose flour
2 cups sugar
4 eggs
1 cup milk
1 cup dried bread crumbs
1/2 lb. candied cherries, diced
1/2 lb. mixed candied peel, diced

1 cup sliced almonds
1/2 cup each grated apple,
    carrots, raw potato
1/2 tsp. each cinnamon, cloves,
    nutmeg, grated lemon rind
1 cup cider
1 cup brandy
3/4 cup molasses
1 tsp. soda

Mix all ingredients except the molasses and soda in a very large mixing bowl. Cover and set in a cool place overnight. Next day add soda to molasses and stir into the batter. For baking, use any of the following containers: a 4-cup glass measure makes the traditional high shape, a Pyrex casserole or bowl with a glass in the

CURRIED FRUIT

This is a nice meat accompaniment for a winter buffet.

1 can (20 ozs.) apricots
1 can (20 ozs.) pineapple chunks
1 can (20 ozs.) pear halves
1 can (20 ozs.) peach halves
1 cup golden raisins

1/3 cup butter
1/2 tsp. curry
3/4 cup brown sugar
10 maraschino cherries, halved
1/2 cup toasted almond halves

Arrange fruit in an 8 x 12-inch glass pan or a large pretty bowl. Melt butter in a 1-cup measure. Stir in curry. Add brown sugar. Microwave 1 minute. Spoon over fruit. Microwave 10 minutes, basting and turning dish several times. Add cherries and nuts just before serving. Serve warm, reheating if necessary. Makes 10 servings.

DESSERTS

A microwave oven is a great asset in preparing many desserts. Cakes, for in stance, are lighter and rise higher. They will not brown, due to the short cookin time, but can be placed under a conventional broiled until browned, if you do no plan to frost them.

Custards and puddings are easier to make. If milk needs to be scalded microwave it one to two minutes per cup. Remember that custard continues to coo after being removed from the oven, so undercook it slightly to prevent separation.

Steamed puddings, instead of taking hours, can be made in ten to fiftee minutes. Use plastic wrap over the container for the steamed effect.

Bar-type cookies are satisfactory, but crisp cookies are best baked conver tionally.

See the chapter on Fruits for several new ideas and the Sauce chapter fo dessert toppings.

center makes a ring shape, or a glass bread pan makes a loaf shape. Flt 2 layers of brown paper into bottoms of molds. Fill molds 2/3 full with the batter. Cover tightly with plastic wrap to get the steamed effect. Microwave 10 to 15 minutes, until top is almost dry and a toothpick comes out clean. The timing depends on the shape and volume of your mold. For best results, bake one at a time and turn as it bakes. To store, wrap in brandy-soaked cheesecloth, then in plastic wrap. Store in a cool place or freeze. To serve, reheat, without unwrapping, in microwave oven 2 to 3 minutes. Unwrap pudding and place on your loveliest serving plate. Dim the lights. Carefully pour warmed brandy over pudding and light. Serve with Golden Sauce on page 42.

*Suet is very easy to grind in a food processor, if your butcher is unwilling to do it for you.

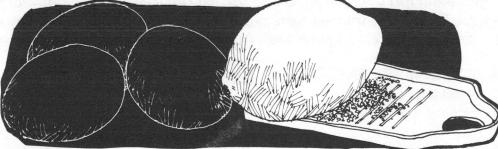

MIMI'S BROWNIES

This family recipe has been around for at least three generations. It is still a favorite.

3 sqs. unsweetened chocolate
1/2 cup butter or margarine
4 eggs
2 cups sugar

1-1/4 cups all-purpose flour
1 tsp. vanilla
pinch salt
1/2 cup chopped nuts

Put the chocolate and butter into a small glass bowl. Microwave 1-1/2 minutes to melt. Cool. Beat eggs with electric mixer until very light, about 5 minutes. Gradually add sugar, then flour, vanilla, salt and melted chocolate. Beat well. Spread in an 8 x 12-inch glass baking dish. Smooth the top. Sprinkle with chopped nuts. Microwave for 7-1/2 minutes, turning 1/4 turn every two minutes. It will puff way up, then settle down as it cools. Cracks are normal. Cut when cool. Makes about 36 bars.

To prevent corners from overcooking, cover each one with a small piece of foil before baking.

EASY CHEESY LEMON BARS

Moist and rich, this bar cookie keeps very well, if lemon-lovers don't discover your supply. Chocolate freaks can substitute devil's food cake mix and fudge frosting.

1/2 cup margarine, melted	1 pkg. (8 ozs.) cream cheese, softened
1 pkg. (18 ozs.) lemon cake mix	1 pkg. (14 ozs.) lemon frosting mix
3 eggs	

Place margarine in a medium sized glass bowl. Microwave 45 seconds, to melt. Add cake mix and 1 slightly beaten egg. Mix with a fork. Place into an 8 x 12-inch glass baking pan or two 8-inch square glass pans. Blend frosting mix into softened cream cheese. Remove and reserve 1/2 cup. Add eggs to remaining frosting mix. Beat 3 to 5 minutes. Spread over cake mixture. Microwave for 5 to 6 minutes at medium (50%) power. Rotate. Microwave for 3 to 5 minutes on high (100%) power. When done, the top will be fairly dry and the sides pulled away from the pan. Do not overcook. Cool. Spread with reserved frosting mix. Cut into small squares. Makes about 40 squares.

SPICY RAISIN COFFEE CAKE

In Grandmother's day this batter made delicious tea cakes. With a microwave oven, it is far easier to make it into a coffee cake.

1/2 cup margarine
2 eggs
1 cup sugar
1 cup (1/2 pt.) sour cream
1 tsp. baking soda

1 cup all-purpose flour
1 tsp. cinnamon
1/4 tsp. cloves
3/4 to 1 cup raisins

Place margarine in a small dish and microwave 1 minute to melt. Beat eggs in large mixing bowl. Slowly beat in sugar. Stir baking soda into sour cream. Add to sugar mixture. Stir in flour, cinnamon, cloves and melted margarine. Spread evenly in an 8-inch square glass pan. Sprinkle raisins over top. Microwave for 5 to 6 minutes at medium (50%) power. Rotate. Microwave for 2 to 3 minutes on high (100%) power. If a deeper color is desired, place under conventional broiler for a minute. Makes 9 servings.

ISLAND CAKE

A moist cake, so good with coffee and especially nice for a brunch.

1/4 cup butter <u>or</u> margarine
1 egg, beaten
1 cup (1/2 pt.) pineapple yogurt
2 cups pancake mix
1/2 cup sugar
3/4 cup shredded coconut
1/2 cup crushed pineapple, well drained

Put butter into a large glass bowl. Microwave 45 seconds until melted. Add beaten egg and yogurt to butter. Stir in remaining ingredients. Spread evenly in an 8 x 12-inch glass pan. Microwave for 4 to 5 minutes on medium (50%) power. Rotate 4 times during this time. Microwave for 2 to 3 minutes on high (100%) power. The cake will continue to bake and the top will dry after being taken from the oven. If a darker color is preferred, place cake under conventional broiler for a minute, or frost with a lemon-flavored, powdered sugar frosting. Makes 8 servings.

GOLDEN CARROT CAKE

Nutritious served as a breakfast variation. Top with a powdered sugar and orange juice glaze for a sweeter version.

1-3/4 cups all-purpose flour
1 cup sugar
1 tsp. baking powder
1 tsp. baking soda
1/2 tsp. salt
1/2 tsp. cinnamon

1/2 tsp. nutmeg
2 eggs
1 cup salad oil
1/2 cup orange juice
1 tsp. vanilla
1 cup shredded carrots

Blend all ingredients in a mixing bowl for three minutes. Turn into an 8 x 12-inch glass pan. Microwave for 5 to 6 minutes on medium (50%) power. Rotate 4 times while cooking. Microwave for 2 to 3 minutes on high (100%) power. Glaze if desired. Cut into squares when cool. Makes 12 servings.

ORANGE GLAZE: Blend together 1 cup powdered sugar and 3 tablespoons orange juice concentrate. Spread on warm cake.

144

SPICY PRUNE CAKE

Here's a deliciously moist cake with a surprise seasoning.

1–1/2 cups cooked prunes
2/3 cup salad oil
1 cup sugar
1/2 cup prune liquid
2 eggs
3 tbs. milk
2 tsp. baking soda

1–2/3 cups all-purpose flour
2 tbs. ground chocolate
1 tsp. allspice
1 tsp. cinnamon
1/2 tsp. salt
2 tsp. vanilla

Finely chop prunes. Mix together oil and sugar. Add prunes and liquid. Add eggs, one at a time, beating well after each addition. Stir in milk, then dry ingredients and vanilla. Spread evenly in an 8 x 12-inch glass pan. Microwave for 5 to 6 minutes on medium (50%) power. Microwave for 2 to 3 minutes on high (100%) power. May be frosted with a light cream cheese frosting, but is also good plain. Makes 1 cake.

POPPY SEED CAKE

Perfect with coffee, this cake improves in flavor if allowed to age.

1 pkg. (18 ozs.) yellow cake mix
1 pkg. (3 ozs.) instant coconut cream pudding mix
1 cup water
1/2 cup salad oil

4 eggs
1/4 cup poppy seed
1/2 cup sherry or fruit juice

Mix all ingredients with an electric mixer for four minutes. Divide into 2 glass 8-inch pans. Microwave each for 4 to 5 minutes on medium (50%) power. Microwave for 2 to 3 minutes on high (100%) power. Turn 1/4 turn every minute four times for more even baking. Frost if desired. Makes two 8- inch cakes.

Frosting spreads easily if the cake has been standing long enough for the surface to dry slightly or if it has been cooled in the refrigerator.

PINEAPPLE UPSIDE-DOWN CAKE

Cake and topping cook all in one—a cinch to please.

2 tbs. butter
1/2 cup brown sugar
1 can (8 ozs.) crushed pineapple,
    drained (reserve juice)

1/2 cup chopped walnuts
2 cups yellow cake mix

Melt butter in an 8-inch round glass pan or 9-inch Corningware skillet. Add brown sugar, pineapple and nuts. Mix together and spread evenly. Prepare cake mix according to package directions, using the reserved pineapple juice for liquid. Add water if necessary. Spread cake batter evenly over the brown sugar mixture. Cover with waxed paper. Microwave for 4 to 5 minutes on medium (50%) power. Rotate 4 times while cooking. Microwave for 2 to 3 minutes on high (100%) power. Remove from oven. Wait 1 minute before turning out on plate or platter. This may be served with whipped cream which has been flavored with lemon rind, vanilla and sugar. Makes 1 cake.

CRAZY MIXED-UP CAKE

1–1/3 cups all-purpose flour
1 cup sugar
3 tbs. cocoa
1 tsp. baking soda
1/2 tsp. salt

1 tsp vanilla
1/4 cup salad oil
1 tbs. vinegar
3/4 cup water or coffee

Sift flour, sugar, cocoa, baking soda and salt into an 8- inch round glass pan. Make three holes. Pour vanilla into one, oil into one, and vinegar into the third. Pour water over all. Stir very, very well with a fork until completely blended. This is the hardest step in making this cake but extremely important. Smooth batter. Microwave for 4 to 5 minutes on medium (50%) power. Rotate 4 times while cooking. Microwave 2 to 3 minutes on high (100%) power. Delicious served plain, dusted with powdered sugar or a la mode. Makes 1 cake.

Cocoa Torte—make 2 layers. Cool. In mixing bowl combine 1 cup whipping cream, 3 tablespoons confectioner's sugar, 2 tablespoons cocoa and 1/4 teaspoon cinnamon. Whip until stiff. Fill and frost top only of cake with mixture.

GINGERBREAD

Here's a modern version of an old-fashioned favorite.

1/4 cup butter <u>or</u> margarine
1/2 cup brown sugar, packed
1 egg
1/2 cup molasses
1–1/2 cups all-purpose flour

1 tsp. baking soda
1 tsp. ginger
1 tsp. cinnamon
1/2 cup buttermilk
Lemon Sauce, page 43

Cream butter and sugar until fluffy. Beat in egg and molasses. Blend spices into the flour. Add to creamed mixture alternately with buttermilk. Pour into an 8 or 9-inch glass pan. Microwave for 4 to 5 minutes on medium (50%) power. Rotate 4 times while cooking. Microwave 2 to 3 minutes on high (100%) power. Cake is done when a toothpick inserted in the middle comes out clean. Serve warm or cold with Lemon Sauce. Makes 6 to 9 servings.

Reheat perked coffee as needed instead of keeping the coffee pot plugged in for hours. Microwave 1–1/2 to 2 minutes per cup or mug.

FRESH PEACH COBBLER

Nothing says summer quite like a fresh fruit cobbler.

4 peaches, peeled and sliced.
3 tbs. sugar
1 tsp. cinnamon
2 cups yellow cake mix*
1/4 cup butter _or_ margarine

Arrange peach slices in an 8-inch square glass pan or a 9-inch Corning skillet. Sprinkle with sugar and cinnamon. Microwave 3 minutes. In a glass bowl, melt butter. Add cake mix. Blend well. Crumble over the peaches. Microwave 10 minutes, turning dish 1/4 turn every two minutes. Cool slightly. Serve with whipped cream or ice cream. Makes 6 to 8 servings.

*Use 1 pkg. (9–1/2 ozs.) one-layer cake mix or 1/2 of a two layer mix. Use leftover mix to make Pineapple Upside-Down Cake, page 147.

TROPICAL PIE

Apple slices poached in pineapple juice give this pie its special flavor!

6 medium apples
1-1/2 cups (12 oz. can) pineapple juice
3/4 cup sugar
3 tbs. cornstarch
1 tbs. butter

1/4 tsp. salt
1 tbs. rum
1/2 cup raisins
One 9-inch pastry shell, baked
whipped cream for garnish

Pare, core and slice apples. Combine 1-1/4 cups juice and sugar in a 1-1/2-quart casserole. Microwave 3 minutes until boiling. Add apple slices. Microwave 7 minutes until just tender. Lift apples from syrup to drain. Combine remaining 1/4 cup juice and cornstarch. Add to syrup. Microwave 4 minutes, stirring often until thickened and bubbly. Add butter, salt, rum and raisins. Cool 10 minutes, uncovered, without stirring. Pour half of the thickened syrup into the baked pie shell. Arrange apples in the pie shell. Pour the rest of the syrup over the apples. Chill several hours or overnight. Garnish with whipped cream before serving. Makes 6 to 8 servings.

PUMPKIN CHIFFON PIE

Nice any time but especially at holiday time when there are many things to do and so little time.

1 envelope Knox unflavored gelatine
1/4 cup cold water
3 eggs
1 cup brown sugar
1 cup canned pumpkin
2 tsp. cinnamon

1/2 tsp. ginger
1/4 tsp. allspice
1/2 tsp. salt
2 tbs. sugar
One 9-inch pastry shell, baked

Soften gelatine in water. Separate eggs. Beat yolks in a small glass mixing bowl. Add sugar and pumpkin. Microwave 4 minutes until thickened. Stir once or twice. Add gelatine and spices. Cool. When mixture begins to congeal, beat egg whites and 2 tablespoons sugar until stiff. Fold in pumpkin mixture. Pour into conventionally baked pie shell and chill several hours. Garnished with whipped cream if desired. Makes one 9-inch pie.

BUTTER PECAN CUPS

A cross between custard and pecan pie and takes less than ten minutes to complete. Scrumptious!

1/4 cup butter
4 eggs
2/3 cup (5.3 ozs.) evaporated milk
1/2 cup sugar

1 cup light Karo corn syrup
1/2 tsp. salt
1 tsp. vanilla
1 cup chopped pecans

Put butter in a small dish and microwave 45 seconds until melted. Beat eggs in mixing bowl. Add evaporated milk, sugar, corn syrup, salt, vanilla and melted butter. Beat well. Divide pecans among six 6-oz. glass custard cups or coffee cups. Pour custard over pecans, dividing evenly. Arrange cups in the oven in a circle with none in the middle. Microwave 7 to 8 minutes until knife inserted in center comes out almost clean. These set more as they cool. Watch as they are cooking and rearrange if necessary for even cooking. Makes 6 servings.

RAISIN RICE PUDDING

Stir up this pudding, and stir up some old-fashioned memories. Perfect for left-over rice.

2 eggs, slightly beaten
1 pkg. (3 ozs.) instant vanilla pudding
2 cups milk
1-1/2 cups rice, cooked
1/2 tsp. vanilla
1/2 cup raisins

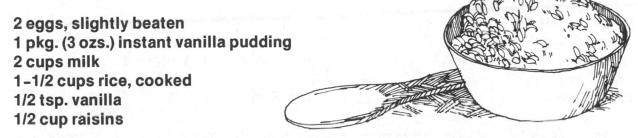

In a glass bowl or 2-1/2-quart Corningware casserole, mix pudding into beaten eggs. Stir in remaining ingredients. Microwave 7 minutes, stirring every two minutes. Cool or chill before serving. Makes 6 servings.

To scald milk, microwave 1-1/2 to 2 minutes on high (100%) power per cup.

PAPPY'S SPECIAL ANGEL TORTE

Light and rich in one bite, this dessert is a favorite for bridge club or party dinners. Make it the day before.

1 envelope unflavored gelatine
1/2 cup cold milk
3 egg yolks, slightly beaten
1–1/2 cups milk
1 cup sugar

1 small angel food cake
3 egg whites, stiffly beaten
1 cup (1/2 pt.) cream, whipped
1/2 tsp. vanilla
Caramel Sauce, page 45

Sprinkle gelatine over 1/2 cup milk to soften. Mix yolks, 1–1/2 cups milk and sugar in a 4-cup glass measure or bowl. Microwave 4 to 5 minutes just until boiling, stirring often after the first two minutes. Add softened gelatine. Cool. Break angel food into pieces (remove crust if desired). Lightly fill a loaf pan or pretty serving casserole with cake pieces. When custard is cool, fold beaten egg whites and cream together. Then fold in custard and vanilla. Pour this mixture over pieces of cake, working it into the spaces. Refrigerate overnight. Serve with Caramel Sauce. Makes 12 servings.

FROZEN GRASSHOPPER TORTE

Keep this in your freezer. Surprise unexpected company.

1/4 cup margarine
30 chocolate wafer cookies, crushed
3 cups miniature marshmallows
3/4 cup milk
1/4 cup green creme de menthe
2 tbs. white cream de cacao
1 cup whipping cream, whipped

To melt margarine, place in a glass bowl and microwave 45 seconds. Stir in wafer crumbs. Put half of mixture into an 8-inch square glass baking dish. Chill. Place marshmallows and milk in a large bowl. Microwave 1-1/2 to 2 minutes, just until marshmallows are melted. Stir in creme de menthe and creme de cacao. Cool. Fold in whipped cream. Pour into crumb-lined dish. Top with remaining crumbs. Freeze until firm. Cut into squares. Makes 9 servings.

HARVEY WALLBANGER CAKE

A bundt pan is used for this "R-rated" delight.

1 pkg. (18–1/2 ozs.) lemon pudding cake mix
   or 1 pkg. orange cake mix plus
   1 sm. pkg. instant vanilla pudding mix
3/4 cup orange juice
1/4 cup vegetable oil

3 eggs
1/4 cup vodka
1/4 cup Galliano liqueur
grated peel of 1 orange
Wallbanger Glaze, next page

Prepare pan according to directions at bottom of next page. Combine all ingredients in a mixer bowl. Mix at medium speed for 4 minutes. Pour batter into bundt pan. Distribute batter evenly. Microwave at medium power (50%) for 8 to 12 minutes. Rotate. Microwave on high power (100%) 2 to 4 minutes, or until toothpick inserted into center comes out clean. Top may still appear moist. Allow to rest for 10 minutes before turning out of pan. Loosen cake around edges with knife. Place plate on top of bundt pan. Invert pan and shake firmly until cake dislodges onto plate. While still warm, drizzle with Wallbanger Glaze.

WALLBANGER GLAZE

1 cup powdered sugar, sifted
1 tbs. orange juice
1-1/2 tsp. Galliano
grated orange peel

Stir all ingredients together in a small mixing bowl. Pour over Harvey Wallbanger cake after it has rested out of the pan about 5 minutes. The cake should just be warm.

> To assure that bundt cakes will invert onto a plate in one piece, spray pan with one of the non-stick products and dust with granulated sugar before adding batter.

SPEEDO FUDGE

This satisfies the sweet tooth as well as the timeclock.

1 lb. powdered sugar
1/2 cup cocoa
1/4 cup milk
1/4 lb. margarine
1 tbs. vanilla
1/2 cup chopped walnuts or pecans

Sift powdered sugar and cocoa into a medium glass mixing bowl. Blend sugar and cocoa. Add milk and margarine but do not stir. Microwave 2 minutes. Add vanilla. Stir just to blend. Pour onto a buttered platter or 8 or 9-inch pan (metal is fine). Sprinkle with nuts. Freeze 20 minutes or chill about 1 hour. Cut when firm. Makes 1-1/4 pounds.

FUDGE FROSTING

The instant coffee can be omitted, but it adds a subtle flavor.

1-1/2 cups brown sugar, packed
4 tbs. cream
1/4 cup butter
2 sq. (2 ozs.) unsweetened chocolate
1 tbs. instant coffee powder
1/2 tsp. vanilla

Put all ingredients into a glass bowl. Microwave 3-1/2 to 4 minutes, stirring frequently. Remove. Beat with electric mixer until thick enough to spread, about 8 minutes. Makes about 2 cups.

Refrigerate or freeze leftover frosting until needed. If refrigerated, microwave 1 to 2 minutes per cup, just to soften. Add a minute or two to the timing, if frozen. Frosting heats quickly because of the high sugar content. Stir well to mix before using.

161

KIDS COOK

At last, children can easily satisfy their curiosity about cooking. While conventional range tops and ovens are complicated and dangerous for a small child to use, a microwave oven is easy to operate and little fingers won't get burned. Once children can read and know how to properly operate a microwave oven, the creations they turn out are surprising.

The fast cooking feature is especially good for children whose patience can reach the breaking point waiting for a cake to bake! And the clean-up becomes so simple there can be no excuses for not doing it.

Children are fascinated watching cupcakes rise and bake in fifteen seconds, caramels and marshmallows melt in a jiffy, or dried oatmeal turn into a delicious bowl of cereal. Because it is fun to make a bowl of soup or other good things in the microwave oven, they will often choose them instead of snacks which are less good for them. It is a fun way to learn about good nutrition.

Let your children plan a party and surprise friends with their own culinary expressions. Before long, they can prepare a meal to please the whole family.

COCOA

Marshmallows taste so good when melted by the hot cocoa!

1 heaping tbs. cocoa mix   3/4 cup milk   2 large marshmallows

Put cocoa mix in a glass, ceramic or heavy plastic mug. Pour in a little milk. Stir until smooth, then add remaining milk. Microwave 1-1/2 minutes. Top with marshmallows. Makes 1 serving.

HOT LEMON TEA

Hot lemon tea warms you up in a hurry on a chilly day!

3/4 cup water   1 tsp. presweetened instant lemon tea mix

Put water in a mug. Microwave 1-1/4 minutes. Add tea mix. Stir. Wait until it cools a bit before drinking. Makes 1 serving.

OATMEAL

What could be better on a frosty winter morning? The brown sugar topping is a special treat. Add a glass of fruit juice, and this breakfast will keep you energized until lunch time.

3/4 cup water
5 tbs. quick cooking oatmeal
dash salt
1 tbs. butter
1 tbs. brown sugar
milk

Measure water, oatmeal and salt into a serving bowl. Stir. Microwave 1-1/2 minutes. Cover. (A small plate makes a good cover.) After a minute or two, stir again. Add butter. When it's almost melted, add brown sugar and as much milk as you like. Makes 1 serving.

To heat milk, microwave 2 to 3 minutes per cup.

GREEN EGGS AND HAM

Dr. Seuss' culinary creation is fit for a celebration. Plan a birthday brunch, or serve up a super-silly supper.

4 eggs
1/4 cup water
1/4 tsp. salt
blue food coloring
1/2 cup chopped ham
4 tsp. butter

Break eggs into a jar with a tight lid. Add milk and salt. Put the lid on and shake very well. Add blue food coloring, one drop at a time. Cover and shake after each addition. When a "lovely" green shade is reached, stop; then add the ham. In a small casserole microwave butter 30 seconds to melt. Add the eggs. Microwave 3 to 4 minutes, stirring very often after the first minute. Cook just until barely set. The eggs will continue to cook and firm up after being removed from the oven. Makes 2 to 4 servings.

TUNA AND MACARONI CASSEROLE

Macaroni and cheese is always a favorite. This dish is so easy even an eight-year-old can prepare it with a little assistance. Add a fruit salad and hot rolls, and your meal is complete.

1 pkg. (7–1/2 ozs.) Golden Grain Macaroni and Cheese
1/4 cup butter or margarine
1/4 cup milk
1 can (6–1/2 ozs.) tuna
1 can (8 ozs.) peas, drained

Have an older person help you cook macaroni in two quarts of rapidly boiling water on top of the stove. It should boil 8 minutes. Drain and place in a 2-quart casserole. Mix in butter, milk, and cheddar cheese mix. Stir in tuna and drained peas. Mix well. Do not cover. Microwave 4 to 5 minutes until bubbly. Allow to rest a few minutes, then serve. Makes 4 servings.

HOT DOGS

Most microwave cookbooks tell you to cook wieners right in the buns, but I prefer this method. Because the paper, rather than the buns, absorbs the fat from the wieners, the hot dogs taste better and are better for you.

1 to 6 buns
1 to 6 wieners

If buns are frozen, defrost them first. Wrap in a paper towel or a small kitchen towel and microwave 10 seconds for each one. Remove from oven. Wrap the same number of wieners tightly in a paper towel. Microwave:

1 wiener — 10 seconds	4 wieners — 45 seconds
2 wieners — 30 seconds	6 wieners — 45 seconds

Place wrapped buns in the oven with the wieners and microwave an additional 30 seconds for 1 to 6 wieners. Do not overcook as the wieners will split and the buns will become tough.

BRAN MUFFINS

Store the batter tightly covered in the refrigerator for up to three weeks. This speedy wholesome treat will be well appreciated on rushed mornings.

4 cups Kellog's All Bran
2 cups Nabisco 100% Bran
1-3/4 cups boiling water
1 qt. buttermilk
3 cups sugar
4 eggs, beaten

1 cup oil
5 cups all-purpose flour
5 tsp. baking soda
1 tsp. salt
1 cup raisins, optional

In a large mixing bowl, mix cereals. Pour water over cereals. Stir until moistened. Add buttermilk, sugar, eggs and oil. Add dry ingredients and raisins. Stir until just combined. To bake, fill paper liners half full. Place in a microwave safe muffin pan or in six individual glass custard cups arranged in a circle. Cook on high for 2 to 3 minutes. For best results, rotate 1/4 turn every minute. Makes 6 dozen.

CUPCAKES

Baking cupcakes presents a problem since the metal pans cannot be used. Cookbooks tell you to use custard cups, but the shape is not so attractive. Here is a novel way to bake traditional-looking cupcakes. Children will need adult help in cutting the molds, but they can be used over again.

 6 styrofoam cups, 7-oz. size
 1 pkg. (18 ozs.) cake mix <u>or</u>
     1 recipe of your favorite batter
 paper cupcake liners

To make cupcake forms, cut the top 1–1/2 inches off the styrofoam cups, using a sharp knife. Discard the bottom part of the cups. Place the rings on a flat plate or platter, or in a glass cake pan. Arrange in a circle with nothing in the middle. Put paper liners inside of the rings. Fill half full with batter. Microwave 15 seconds for each cupcake being baked. Six cupcakes take about 1–1/2 minutes. Watch as they bake. It's fun to see how quickly they rise. They are done when a toothpick comes out clean. Some of the tops may look a little wet, but since there is additional cook-

ing after the cupcakes are removed from the oven, do not cook longer than the 1-1/2 minutes. They will dry as they cool. And do not try to bake more than six at a time. (Leftover batter may be stored, tightly covered, in the refrigerator. Stir well before using and add 5 seconds to the cooking time.) Cool cupcakes before frosting. Makes about 40.

CUPCAKE CONES

A novel way to celebrate a child's birthday or surprise the Scouts at their next meeting.

1 pkg. (17 ozs.) cake mix, any flavor
24 to 30 flat bottom ice cream cones

Prepare your favorite cake mix as the package directs. Fill cones with 2 table-spoons batter, about half full. Baking 6 cones at a time, microwave 1 to 1-1/4 minutes until a toothpick inserted in the center comes out clean. Frost with whipped cream or frosting, and decorate with colored sprinkles if desired. Makes 24 to 30.

Give store-bought or leftover cookies a "fresh from the oven" flavor. Place about a dozen cookies at a time, in a circle, on a paper plate. Microwave 1 minute until just barely warm.

ROCKY ROAD BROWNIES

You may begin with your favorite brownie recipe, but it is easier to start with a mix.

1 pkg. (22 ozs.) brownie mix
2 cups miniature marshmallows
1 sq. (1 oz.) unsweetened chocolate
2 tbs. margarine

1 tsp. vanilla
dash salt
2 cups powdered sugar
1/4 cup water

Prepare brownie mix according to package directions. Spoon into an 8 x 12-inch pan and smooth the top. Microwave 6 minutes. Remove from the oven. Sprinkle marshmallows over the top. Cool. Put chocolate and margarine into a glass bowl. Microwave 1 minute to melt. Add remaining ingredients and beat. Carefully spread frosting over the marshmallows. Cut into bars when cool. Makes 48 bars.

> Ice cream taken from the freezer can be softened enough to easily scoop. Microwave 30 to 45 seconds per pint.

PETER PANS

When Wendy brought these to her Brownie meeting, they disappeared faster than her leader could say "Tinkerbell." You'll love them too.

1 pkg. (6 ozs.) chocolate chips
1 pkg. (6 ozs.) butterscotch chips
1/2 cup margarine
3/4 cup peanut butter
2 cups miniature marshmallows
6 ozs. Planter's peanuts

Put chips, margarine and peanut butter into an 8- x 12-inch glass baking dish. Microwave 2 to 3 minutes until everything is melted. Stir well. Cool, then add marshmallows and peanuts. Refrigerate. When firm, cut into small squares. Makes 48 or more pieces.

GLOSSARY OF MICROWAVE TERMS

Adapting or converting: changing conventional recipes to work in a microwave oven.

Arcing: flashes of light seen if metal is used in the microwave oven.

Arranging: the placement of food, in a circle when possible, for best cooking results.

Automatic temperature control: a built-in probe in some ovens which allows cooking to a specific temperature rather than cooking by time.

Browning: occurs naturally when cooking more than three pounds or for more than ten minutes. Special products may be brushed on foods for a browned appearance, or hot food may be placed under a broiler very briefly.

Browning skillet or tray: a ceramic utensil with a coating of tin oxide which, when preheated, becomes hot, allowing food placed on it to brown before cooking.

Carry-over cooking time, resting, holding: the time after the cooking period when food reaches its optimum temperature.

Cooking grill or rack: usually made of high temperature resistant plastic, it allows moisture and fat to drain. Also useful for defrosting frozen foods and baking cakes and brownies.

Covers: see special section for explanation, page 5

Delicate foods: eggs, cheese, seafood, milk; foods which cook best on reduced power settings.

Densities: affect the rate at which a food will cook. Porous foods, such as bread and casseroles cook more quickly than dense foods, such as meat.

High altitude: may need slightly longer time but no other adjustment to recipe.

Piercing: the poking of a food to allow steam to escape and prevent an explosion.

Shielding: using a small piece of foil on thin areas or corners of square or rectangular pans to redirect the microwaves and allow more even cooking.

Stirring: bringing uncooked portions from the middle to the outside and pushing cooked portions to the middle. This is especially necessary in microwave cooking of casseroles and eggs.

Turning, turn over, rotate: a technique to assure the most even cooking by flipping the food over to equalize penetration by microwaves. The need for rearranging and rotating has been eliminated by new technology being employed by some oven manufacturers. Check your oven manual to learn if you can eliminate these steps.

INDEX

METRIC CONVERSION CHART

Liquid or Dry Measuring Cup (based on an 8 ounce cup)

1/4 cup = 60 ml
1/3 cup = 80 ml
1/2 cup = 125 ml
3/4 cup = 190 ml
1 cup = 250 ml
2 cups = 500 ml

Liquid or Dry Measuring Cup (based on a 10 ounce cup)

1/4 cup = 80 ml
1/3 cup = 100 ml
1/2 cup = 150 ml
3/4 cup = 230 ml
1 cup = 300 ml
2 cups = 600 ml

Liquid or Dry Teaspoon and Tablespoon

1/4 tsp. = 1.5 ml
1/2 tsp. = 3 ml
1 tsp. = 5 ml
3 tsp. = 1 tbs. = 15 ml

Temperatures

°F		°C
200	=	100
250	=	120
275	=	140
300	=	150
325	=	160
350	=	180
375	=	190
400	=	200
425	=	220
450	=	230
475	=	240
500	=	260
550	=	280

Pan Sizes (1 inch = 25 mm)

8-inch pan (round or square) = 200 mm x 200 mm
9-inch pan (round or square) = 225 mm x 225 mm
9 x 5 x 3-inch loaf pan = 225 mm x 125 mm x 75 mm
1/4 inch thickness = 5 mm
1/8 inch thickness = 2.5 mm

Pressure Cooker

100 Kpa = 15 pounds per square inch
70 Kpa = 10 pounds per square inch
35 Kpa = 5 pounds per square inch

Mass

1 ounce = 30 g
4 ounces = 1/4 pound = 125 g
8 ounces = 1/2 pound = 250 g
16 ounces = 1 pound = 500 g
2 pounds = 1 kg

Key   (America uses an 8 ounce cup - Britain uses a 10 ounce cup)

ml = milliliter
l = liter
g = gram
K = Kilo (one thousand)
mm = millimeter
m = milli (a thousandth)
°F = degrees Fahrenheit

°C = degrees Celsius
tsp. = teaspoon
tbs. = tablespoon
Kpa = (pounds pressure per square inch)
    This configuration is used for pressure cookers only.

Metric equivalents are rounded to conform to existing metric measuring utensils.